PRAISE FOR THE PLAYS

NOCTURNE

"A startling, unnerving work of art that fiercely pushes the boundaries of theater . . . Rapp is an original—a distinctive voice . . . *Nocturne* will haunt you for a long time."
—MICHAEL KUCHWARA, Associated Press

"A brilliant, terrifying, perceptive, occasionally funny play . . . Bold, daring and successful." —DONALD LYONS, *New York Post*

"Adam Rapp's *Nocturne* is remarkable enough to bear comparisons with Margaret Edson's award-winning *Wit* . . . Here [is] a playwright . . . to watch with keen interest."
—MARKLAND TAYLOR, *Variety*

"At once beautiful and haunting, compelling and agonizing . . . A bold, elegant and even funny exploration of how a single moment has the power to both connect us and change our lives."
—MARK DE LA VIÑA, *San Jose Mercury News*

STONE COLD DEAD SERIOUS

"Rapp is very gifted, and, even rarer, he has something to say . . . *Stone Cold Dead Serious* [is] brave, compassionate and, at times . . . breathtakingly moving."
—BRUCE WEBER, *The New York Times*

"Sharp and disquieting . . . Beneath the scurrilous comic banter and absurd surfaces is a mysterious recurrence of objects, actions, personae and language, in an oblique and haunting style reminiscent of Haruki Murakami's best fiction . . . *Stone Cold Dead Serious* works as a kind of venomous sustenance, dangerous but invigorating." —ED PARK, *The Village Voice*

"Will leave your mind buzzing and your heart aching."
—BRANDON WOLCOTT, *Show*

"[A] scabrous, poignant vision of suburban-American innocence lost." —CAROLYN CLAY, *The Boston Phoenix*

FASTER

"Talented and highly prolific . . . Rapp . . . is brave and facile in his language, and he ventures [in *Faster*] where few writers are able or willing to go." —BRUCE WEBER, *The New York Times*

"There's no want of energy [in] *Faster* . . . [Rapp] has a rising reputation for creating fast-talking, hard-hitting characters who make up in colorful language and intensity of physical connection what they lack in, well, social graces."
—JEREMY GERARD, *New York*

"[Rapp] has made a name for himself writing about the darker things . . . *Faster* is no exception as it examines the complex relationship between hope and reality, faith and circumstance."
—RANEE JABER, *Show Business Weekly*

"The most anticipated and talked about play [at the 2002 Louisville Humana Festival]."   —*Back Stage*

"The[se] aren't your typical alienated hipsters. Mr. Rapp is aiming for something much more grand and metaphysical than just another mundane tale of arrested development."
—JASON ZINOMAN, *The New York Times*

"Rapp boldly and honestly exposes a segment of society that most of us, thankfully, know only from a distance. [*Finer Noble Gases*] is a resounding warning about what happens when parents disconnect from their children and the young turn to drugs, television and other substances as emotional pacifiers."
—JUDITH EGERTON, *The Courier-Journal* (Louisville)

"Rockers Chase . . . and Staples . . . are a present-day Vladimir and Estragon—hoboes with nowhere to go, waiting indefinitely for someone to rescue them . . . [and] given Rapp's view of slackerdom as a kind of installation art, [the play] helps turn what feels like nothing into something of hypnotic beauty."
—DAVID NG, *The Village Voice*

ADAM RAPP

RED LIGHT WINTER

Adam Rapp has been the recipient of the Herbert & Patricia
Brodkin Scholarship; two Lincoln Center le Compte de Nuoy
Awards; a fellowship to the Camargo Foundation in Cassis,
France; the 1999 Princess Grace Award for Playwriting; a 2000
Roger L. Stevens Award from the Kennedy Center Fund for New
American Plays; a 2000 Suite Residency with Mabou Mines;
the 2001 Helen Merrill Award for Emerging Playwrights; and
Boston's Elliot Norton Award. He was short-listed for the 2003
William Saroyan International Prize for Writing for *Nocturne* and
received the Jeff Award for Best New Work in 2005 for *Red Light
Winter*.

His plays include *Ghosts in the Cottonwoods* (Victory Gardens;
The Arcola, London); *Animals and Plants* (American Repertory
Theatre); *Blackbird* (The Bush, London; Pittsburgh City Theatre;
Off-Broadway at Edge Theater); *Nocturne* (A.R.T.; Off-Broadway
at New York Theatre Workshop); *Stone Cold Dead Serious* (A.R.T.;
Off-Broadway at Edge Theater); *Finer Noble Gases* (26th Annual
Humana Festival of New American Plays; Off-Broadway at
Rattlestick); *Faster* (Off-Broadway at Rattlestick); *Trueblinka*

(Off Broadway at the Maverick Theater); *Dreams of the Salthorse* (Encore, San Francisco); and *Gompers* (Pittsburgh City Theatre; The Arcola, London).

His first anthology of plays, *Plays by Adam Rapp*, was published by Broadway Play Publishing. His new collection of plays, *Stone Cold Dead Serious and Other Plays*, is available in a trade edition by Faber and Faber, as is *Nocturne*.

His first feature film, *Winter Passing*, starring Ed Harris, Will Ferrell, and Zooey Deschanel, which he wrote and directed, premiered at the 2005 Toronto International Film Festival.

He is the author of the young adult novels *Missing the Piano* (Viking/HarperCollins), *The Buffalo Tree* (Front Street/HarperCollins), *The Copper Elephant* (Front Street/HarperCollins), *33 Snowfish* (Candlewick Press), and *Under the Wolf, Under the Dog* (Candlewick Press), which was short-listed for the Los Angeles Times Book Prize.

He is currently at work on a graphic novel, *Decelerate Blue*, forthcoming from First Second, and the adult novel *The Year of Endless Sorrows*, which will be published by Farrar, Straus and Giroux.

A graduate of Clarke College in Dubuque, Iowa, Rapp also completed a two-year playwriting fellowship at Julliard. He lives in New York City.

RED LIGHT WINTER

FABER AND FABER, INC.

An affiliate of Farrar, Straus and Giroux

NEW YORK

RED LIGHT WINTER

A PLAY BY

ADAM RAPP

FABER AND FABER, INC.
An affiliate of Farrar, Straus and Giroux
19 Union Square West, New York 10003

Distributed in Canada by Douglas & McIntyre Ltd.
Printed in the United States of America
First edition, 2006

Grateful acknowledgment is made for permission to reprint lines from
"Bastards of Young," words and music by Paul Westerberg, copyright © 1995
WB Music Corp. and Nah Music. All rights administered by WB Music Corp.
All rights reserved. Used by permission.

Library of Congress Control Number: 2005931564
ISBN-13: 978-0-86547-954-8
ISBN-10: 0-86547-954-2

Designed by Gretchen Achilles

www.fsgbooks.com

5   7   9   10   8   6   4

FOR WALT

ACKNOWLEDGMENTS

Heartfelt thanks go out to Carl Mulert, who stuck by me for seven years and convinced the powers that be at Steppenwolf—particularly the artistic director, Martha Lavey—that I was up to the task of directing my own work. Ed Sobel, literary manager, also was very helpful in guiding me toward some tough cuts. I must point out as well that I had a terrific design team for the Steppenwolf production, which was anchored by Todd Rosenthal's stunning set and Keith Parham's haunting lighting. Michelle Tesdall's costumes perfectly looked like real clothes from a closet.

I would also like to thank Tim Sanford of Playwrights Horizons for commissioning me, John Buzzetti for helping guide the play to New York, Julien Thuan for his constant support of my strange career, and Scott Rudin, Robyn Goodman, and Stuart Thompson for making the Off-Broadway production a reality.

Finally, I want to thank Dallas Roberts, Ty Burrell, Annie Parisse, Amelia Warner, Ebon Moss-Bachrach, and Zooey Deschanel for performing various readings of the play during its development. And I especially want to thank Lisa Joyce, Gary Wilmes, and Christopher Denham for their fearless work and faith in me.

HOTELS AND HOSTELS

I started writing *Red Light Winter* when I was supposed to be doing other things. I was in Los Angeles for a few days, meeting with actors about a film project I was trying to put together, and feeling very pale and incredibly out of place. While in the lounge of a swanky hotel that I could never afford, waiting for an actress to arrive, I started daydreaming about a brief time I spent in Amsterdam with an old friend, some five years before. I have no idea why memories of Amsterdam were suddenly haunting me. Perhaps I was in some state of West Coast–induced angst over the intimidating prospect of embarking as a playwright on a film project and it prompted an out-of-body experience so extreme that I imaginatively projected myself as far away from L.A. as possible— so far away that I flew over New York, the Atlantic, and back in time no less, landing in the Netherlands. Maybe it was some random pheromone wafting through the lobby. Or maybe it was a good old-fashioned dose of creative denial. (I have to admit that I had been dreading being tagged yet another emerging playwright who was "selling out" to the West Coast.)

What happened in Amsterdam was this: My best friend, Wilhelm, and I had just arrived there with the typical postgraduate American male agenda: to spend five days partying and sitting around in cafés, smoking pot and drinking cheap Heineken and sleeping in hostels and going to "alternative" museums. And for Wilhelm, I was also going to purchase a session with a Red Light District prostitute. I should point out that Wilhelm hadn't been with a woman in over three and a half years, and that he had lost his confidence after his ex had left him while he was living in Japan, teaching English to middle school children. They had been living together on Avenue A, and when he returned at the end of the semester, she had moved out, sold their furniture, and changed the locks, never to be heard from again. It was enough to drive anyone's confidence into the nearest foxhole. So I was determined to get Wilhelm back on the proverbial horse.

It was the late fall of 1997, when the guilder was still the mode of Dutch currency and the services of one of these Red Light District ladies could be purchased pretty reasonably. After a few rounds of beers and lots of coaxing, Wilhelm finally agreed to the plan under one condition: that I sleep with a window prostitute as well, and more specifically, that I partake of that same prostitute's services first. Why Wilhelm was so insistent on me going first eludes me to this day. And why he wanted to be with the same woman is equally baffling. I cite all of this not to boast of my wild late twenties (it had been a while since I'd been with anyone as well), but rather to illustrate the complex extracurricular triangle I was about to become the hypotenuse of. I'd never been one to shy away from mini-adventures, so I downed the rest of my pint, cleaned up a little, and went "shopping."

The strip of Red Light District windows was only a few blocks away from our hostel. I was surprised at how young and beautiful many of these window women were, dressed in white lace, high heels, and garters. It was odd being one of many tourists (and predominantly American tourists at that) walking along the channels as if we were on the promenade of some dimly lit, risqué theme park. After a few minutes, I made eye contact with one. She was very pretty, with dark hair and big brown eyes. I walked over to her, she opened a door next to the window, and a few minutes later my clothes were off and we were having uneventful, rather clinical sex, which was initiated by the application of the thickest condom I have ever seen or worn in my life. Her name was actually Christina and she was purportedly a Greek medical student hooking to earn tuition during the holiday break.

Before we began she pressed a button on a portable cassette player that was secured to the headboard and Tom Waits's *Rain Dogs* issued forth. (I kept Waits, but changed it to *Small Change*— my favorite record of his.) I have to admit that I was intrigued by the bizarre circumstances: here I was in the tiny cell-like room of an exotic prostitute, with only a set of velvet drapes and a storefront window separating me from the throngs of tourists. The queen-size bed with its institutional white linens and sturdy mattress dominated the space. Getting my clothes off was like trying to negotiate a ten-speed bike through a subway turnstile. Christina lit candles and incense and, led by her broken English, we spoke for a few minutes about where I was from and where she was from and how long I was in town for and what I did for a living (inexplicably, I told her I was a concert pianist, which is a gross personal fiction). She certainly made me feel comfortable enough, but for some reason I wasn't able to reach orgasm (I'm sure all the space cakes didn't help either), so I stopped, removed the said extra-strength piece of contraception, dressed, paid the seventy guilders fee plus a decent tip, and then offered up another seventy guilders as a guarantee, explaining that I was going to return with my friend. Christina accepted the money and seemed fine with the whole idea, so I went back and got Wilhelm, who had been reading a Lawrence Durrell novel and drinking his fourth or fifth Heineken. After a brief introduction I left him at the window.

A few hours later he returned to the lobby of our hostel with a big smile on his face and a bit of a swagger. He spent the next hour or so chronicling over beers the details of what went down. It turned out that he had actually paid for an additional two sessions with Christina out of his own pocket. According to Wilhelm, the first session understandably went pretty quickly, and the second session was more of a groove thing during which he rediscovered his racing legs. The majority of the third and final session was spent post-coitally snuggling and talking about childhoods, the Greek seaside, and Tom Waits. I could definitely sense that they had made a connection, or at least one of them had.

As it turns out, Wilhelm and I did try to see Christina the following day, just to say goodbye before boarding our train to Paris, but she was not in her window; a Nordic-looking blonde with pale skin and eerie green eyes had taken her place. Christina was gone and that was that.

But the story actually gets a little more complicated from there. Wilhelm and I did take that train to Paris, and a few days later we both fell for the same girl, whom we met in an Australian bar while playing gin. Impossibly named Holy, she was from Madagascar and very independent and beautiful, with long black hair and almond-shaped eyes, and she wound up liking me and not my friend. This put a strain on the rest of our travels, which would conclude that week. Realizing it only now as I am writing this, in some ways, I must have conflated the two women in the Christina of *Red Light Winter*, because although I didn't feel anything more than physiological friction for the real Christina, I did wind up getting quite attached to Holy, and it was my experience with her that feeds some of the ambiguities that exist in the fiction that became the play.

So for some reason, while I was waiting for my meeting in the lobby of that fancy hotel in Los Angeles, that's where my mind retreated. The notion of writing a complicated love triangle that started with two men sleeping with the same woman seemed an intriguing subject, one that I hadn't taken a crack at before.

I took my notebook out and started writing immediately. When the actress whom I was to meet finally arrived, I had already found my way into that hostel room and I was off and running. Four and a half days later I had finished act one.

A few days later I went to the O'Neill Playwrights Conference, where for a month I was to be a playwright in residence, which basically meant hanging out and eating a lot of cafeteria food. With its extended lawns and foggy sea air and all the great writers who had worked there, the O'Neill is perhaps one of the most inspiring environments for any playwright. It was the perfect place to delve into the second act and complete a draft, which I did in about a week. Leaping forward a year, I set Act II in the SRO apartment of Matt, the quiet, slightly nebbishy, perpetually emerging playwright who had fallen in love with Christina, the prostitute whom his best friend, Davis, had purchased for him in Amsterdam the previous winter. So while it certainly borrowed from real life, the story took on its own dimensions. I wanted to be sure, for instance, that Matt and Davis didn't directly correspond to my friend and me, as what interested me most was dealing with the dynamics of a double-unrequited love triangle, one in which Matt falls in love with Christina, who in turn falls in love with Davis, who—and this is the complicated part—pretends *not* to fall in love with Christina in order to preserve his friendship with Matt. Complicated, I know, but the gray areas intrigued me: how we hold on to the tiniest details when we encounter someone we're bewitched by, and how the other person might not remember the most obvious things from that meeting; the cruelty and pain of being disremembered versus the alchemy of selective memory and how we twist and distort it to rationalize and justify what we want to believe about the object of our affection; how we misinterpret minutiae and mythologize the most insignificant looks and lilts of the voice; how the most meaningless actions can carry enormous, existentially romantic impact. The more I wrote the more interesting the ambiguities were, and I realized that the crux of my play lay in them.

Toward the end of the residency, I read the first act of the play in front of the conference and got a lot of good feedback, making me anxious to hear some actors take a crack at it. I should add that at that time Playwrights Horizons had given me my second full-length commission (my first was from the Pittsburgh City Theatre for my play *Gompers*), and I was excited about giving this play to them. The artistic director, Tim Sanford, despite liking *Red Light Winter*, wound up passing on it, which was a major disappointment for me. Nevertheless, my enthusiasm for the play never waned and I directed a reading of it at the Manhattan Theatre Club Mondays at 6 reading series, which went very well. A few months later, Martha Lavey from Steppenwolf called me. I happened to be in Chicago (I was actually at a Cubs game when she phoned), and she asked me to come to her office that afternoon to discuss the play. I was almost shocked to discover that Martha Lavey was seriously considering the play for their Garage Theatre, even after I insisted on directing it (I'd grown weary of other directors distorting my work). Not only did she not flinch, she supported the idea. This would mark the first time that Steppenwolf had ever allowed a playwright to direct his or her own work, and I didn't want to let them down.

I cast Gary Wilmes in the role of Davis, the charming sexual carnivore who was on a fast track as a young editor darling in the New York book publishing world. On paper, Davis can come off as being almost pathologically cruel, and I knew I had to cast someone with acres of charm; someone who could seduce anyone at any time with his wit, sex appeal, and good looks. Otherwise he's dismissible by minute five. Davis is a psychological daredevil and a narcissist who is diseased by the idea that he can love any woman on any given night and that it is an authentic experience.

But it can only last for a finite period of time, for those few glistening hours, before he tires of his victim and moves on to the next conquest. In some ways, he's a collector of seduction anecdotes, but he wants to believe that he's actually falling in love over and over and over again. Gary, whom I had seen in a few of Richard Maxwell's plays, was a perfect choice, as he possesses the unique combination of an almost overwhelmingly deep reservoir of intelligent yet goofy charm (I spent perhaps 30 percent of the rehearsal process laughing at him), and a cutting, rigorously unsentimental fearlessness about being a bastard.

Matt, Davis's insecure college buddy from Brown who hasn't been with a woman in over three years, is a struggling, insomnia-addled, sparingly awarded playwright with a penchant for isolation and a rather large appetite for antihistamines. Paradoxically, he also possesses a fierce love for writers like Henry Miller, John Fante, and Frederick Exley, writers who lived out unusual, risky lives and wrote about it. At the top of the play he's on the verge of suicide. Christopher Denham, also a talented up-and-coming playwright, was the perfect choice. He had an incredible command of not only the linguistic gymnastics (he has at least three sparingly punctuated arias), but also came prepared with a potent under-standing of what it's like to live with an intense emotional wound that has never healed.

For Christina, I hired a young actress named Lisa Joyce, a grad-uate of the DePaul program. I don't like auditioning actors, as I find the process incredibly condescending. I've also learned that successful auditions rarely have anything to do with whether actors are good to work with, how they make use of a monthlong process, or what kind of storyteller they are. But I had to hire a local woman for the role, and I didn't know very many actresses who were based in Chicago, so I saw over forty women in a span of two days. Lisa simply blew me away and I was stunned to discover that she was only recently out of school. In the play, Christina has a slippery identity. Like Matt, she is incredibly lonely, although she would never admit it in the way he would, and continually re-invents herself as a means to survive. I needed an actress who could convey all this as well as one who could sing and speak English with a convincing French accent. Lisa was able to almost shape-change with the various movements of the play.

So I was fortunate to have a very talented cast. We had a little over three and a half weeks to get the play ready for tech. I don't know that I've ever had a more fulfilling rehearsal process. I find that when I direct my own work, I am a more rigorous storyteller in that I become much more of an audience advocate. As the playwright in the corner, I don't care so much about what anyone thinks, and I often wind up either frustrated with where things are heading or I start daydreaming about another play. As a director, I want the audience to be involved in every moment, which makes me examine every beat of the script in a much more thorough way. So I also become something of a relentless dramaturge. Moreover, I love to work with creative actors who bring bold choices into the room. As many actors whom I've worked with know, I'm a control freak about the words (I demand syllable-perfect performances, as all playwrights worth their salt should), but I actually love rediscovering moments, and allowing the actors to author their roles with me. Gary and I discovered his kung fu entrances and a ton of unspoken bits that helped to amp up the tension. Lisa brought a sense of humor and playfulness to Christina that gave a much-needed buoyancy to the play. Chris's self-deprecating delivery, the way he could throw text away and still have a strong current of thought underneath what remained, and the way he could simply observe the private connections between Davis and Christina, inspired me to really dig into those moments, and ulti-mately all of it became clearly sourced into the text.

The Steppenwolf production wound up being a great success. It was the first play in their history to completely sell out the Garage Theatre. It was also extended for two weeks and nominated for two Joseph Jefferson Citations: one for Best New Work, and one for Best Supporting Actress (Lisa Joyce).

The play for me is certainly laced with tragedy. I think there is a pervasive, almost disabling, melancholic loneliness that puts a great deal of fear in my own heart; and perhaps this is why I wrote the thing: to somehow come up with the antidote for my own worries about winding up old and alone. The two people who probably need each other the most wind up missing their opportunity. I'll leave it for you to figure out whom I mean. But with the sorrow, I think there is a glimmer of hope. The character left listening to Tom Waits's "Jitterbug Boy" at the end of the play might snap out of a terrible funk and find a way out of that little room with the snowy window.

For me the play is also about how complicated a close friendship can be: how the people we care about the most can also be our worst enemies and why even the most unhealthy friendship can have an irrational, long-standing history. Recently, my editor, in thinking about the play, reminded me of the great Replacements song "Bastards of Young" from their album *Tim*. I think they capture it best with the following verse: "The ones who love us best / are the ones we'll lay to rest / and visit their graves on holidays at best. / The ones who love us least / are the ones we'll die to please. / If it's any consolation, I don't begin to understand them."

After writing a bunch of plays, some good and some very bad, I've come to learn that I'm perhaps in my most interesting territory when that being-seized-by-the-throat feeling occurs and I feel the heart-racing panic that makes me drop everything, grab the nearest pen, and start writing. I'm glad I had that notebook handy while I was waiting to meet that actress in the lobby of that Los Angeles hotel. Because for me, a play can be like a fitful bird (or is it a squirrel?) that lands next to me for the briefest moment, if I don't catch it that exact second I'll lose it forever.

ADAM RAPP
September 2005

RED LIGHT WINTER

Red Light Winter was originally produced in Chicago, Illinois, by the Steppenwolf Theatre Company on May 30, 2005. It was directed by Adam Rapp; sets were designed by Todd Rosenthal; costumes by Michelle Tesdell; lights by Keith Parham; and sound by Andre Pluess and Ben Sussman. The production stage manager was Kerry Epstein. The assistant director was Joanie Schultz. The cast was as follows:

MATT	*Christopher Denham*
DAVIS	*Gary Wilmes*
CHRISTINA	*Lisa Joyce*

Red Light Winter was subsequently produced in New York City by Scott Rudin, Robyn Goodman, Stuart Thompson, and Scott Morfee at the Barrow Street Theatre in January 2006. It was directed by Adam Rapp; sets were designed by Todd Rosenthal; costumes by Michelle Tesdell; lights by Keith Parham; and sound by Eric Shim. The production stage manager was Richard A. Hodge. The cast was as follows:

MATT	*Christopher Denham*
DAVIS	*Gary Wilmes*
CHRISTINA	*Lisa Joyce*

CHARACTERS

MATT   *thirty*

DAVIS   *thirtyish*

CHRISTINA   *twenty-five*

SETTING

Amsterdam and New York City

ACT I

A nondescript, inexpensive hostel room in Amsterdam's Red Light
District, not too far from the train station. Two made twin beds, one
upstage center, one downstage right. Tall, blank walls, with a small
shelf over the downstage-right bed. A small lamp hangs from the shelf.
Also on the shelf is a paperback dictionary and random toiletries. On
the upstage wall, three coat hooks. A door leading to a hallway. An
offstage bathroom just outside the door. Above the upstage bed, a window
overlooks the street below. There are two duffel bags, whose contents are
half unpacked. There is a desk next to the window. On the desk, a
laptop computer, some pens. It is winter.

MATT is seated at the desk. He is thin, boyish, a little nervous, slightly
unkempt, an insomniac. His dress is somewhat nondescript. His pants
are just pants. His shoes are just shoes. He wears a long-sleeved thermal
undershirt under a plain brown T-shirt. He is peering at his computer
screen. He has been this way for a long time.

It is early evening. The light from the hostel sign spills in weakly through
the window.

After a moment, MATT pushes away from the desk and stands. He stares
at a hook on the wall. He then walks to the center of the room, paces a
bit, removes his belt while pacing, stops, stands very still. He pulls on the
belt a few times to test its weight-bearing possibilities. He turns to the desk,
studies it for a moment, crosses to the chair, centers it to the desk, and
aligns his computer and pens symmetrically. He then turns the desk lamp
off, considers this light, turns the lamp back on. He crosses back to the

center of the room, feeds the belt through the buckle, and loops it over his head and around his neck. He tugs on the end of the belt a few times, creating a noose, which produces a few gagging sounds. With the belt noosed around his neck, he then approaches the wall, forces a belt hole over the hook, squats so that the belt is stiff with tension, breathes extremely rapidly for a moment, and then lifts his feet, attempting to hang himself. The hook breaks and MATT *crashes to the floor just as the sound of keys jingling on the other side of the door can be heard.*

MATT *desperately undoes the belt from around his neck and stands very quickly, hiding the belt, just as the door opens.*

DAVIS *enters with the flair of a high-energy kung-fu movie. He performs a series of kicks and punches, making kung-fu noises—a typical* DAVIS *entrance. He is standing on one of the beds and the overhead room light is on now as he punctuates his entrance. He leaves the door open. He is broad-shouldered, handsome, clean-shaven, confident, a charmer. He wears conservative, casual attire and a smart winter coat. Throughout the following,* DAVIS *crosses to the shelf above his bed, grabs deodorant, applies it, gets a clean pair of underwear out of his bag, stuffs it in his pocket.* MATT *remains standing, awkwardly holding on to the belt.*

DAVIS You're missing all the fun, bro. This place is a trip. It's totally familiar but dreamlike at the same time. The cobblestone streets. The velvet curtains in the sex windows. Cyclers riding their three-speeds into crowds of pedestrians. Silver mimes pop-locking for spare change. It's like a fucking Tim *Burton* movie or something.

From the shelf DAVIS *grabs a cylinder of some sort of scented aerosol musk, sprays a few clouds into the air and walks into them. When* DAVIS *isn't looking,* MATT *works the hook back into the wall.*

ADAM RAPP

DAVIS There's this homeless guy over by the Anne Frank museum who I swear I've seen in the East Village. He wears a lab coat. Pushes a duck around in a shopping cart. Same coat. Same duck. Bits of electric tape in his beard. It's like some slightly refracted parallel reality.

MATT It's the heroin.

DAVIS What heroin—I haven't done any heroin.

MATT No, some guy in Paris told me there's this um sect of addicts that revolves between the East Village, Zurich, and Amsterdam. They follow the quality stuff around. This dealer supports their habit pro bono for talking up the product in the streets. Flies them business class from city to city. He's revered as this like total holy man.

DAVIS Talk about direct marketing.

MATT The guy with the duck probably is the same guy from the East Village.

DAVIS You know who I'm talking about?

MATT Yeah, bits of electric tape twisted in his beard. He used to hang out by the ATM at Banco Popular and like quote Schopenhauer all the time. I think his name is Saigon.

DAVIS Yeah, Saigon. That's the guy.

DAVIS *spritzes* MATT *with the cylinder of musk.* MATT *flinches and lowers his computer screen.* DAVIS *crosses to the door.*

DAVIS It's such a fucking trip. It makes the world feel so small. I mean, migrating marketeering junkies, who would've thought? By the way . . . (*he points to someone who has been waiting in the hall*) this is Christina.

He beckons her in. CHRISTINA *enters. She is beautiful, pale, somehow lost. She wears a too-thin coat; a sweater underneath, with a coffee*

*stain; a knit hat; a scarf; and mittens, and she carries a large baglike
purse. Despite the dark makeup, her eyes make you forget what day it is.
She is generally quiet but when she does speak she uses a French accent.*

DAVIS Christina, Matt.

MATT *stands, approaches her. They shake.*

CHRISTINA Nice to meet you.
MATT Nice to meet you.

They watch each other for a moment and then MATT *crosses to his bed,
where he attempts to gracefully kick his underwear, socks, and used towel
out of sight.* DAVIS *removes* CHRISTINA's *coat.* MATT *attempts to cross
back to the desk, but* DAVIS *cuts him off at the pass and* MATT *backs up
and sits on the downstage bed.* DAVIS *sits with* CHRISTINA *on the upstage
bed. An awkward pause.* DAVIS *shoots* MATT *a look to urge him on.*

MATT So, how is it out there?
DAVIS Cold. But it's weird. You don't feel it as much here.
MATT You might want to lay off the space cakes.
DAVIS No, I'm serious. Temperature-wise it's as bad as New York
    but it feels somehow milder. Even when the wind hits you it's
    sort of soothing.

CHRISTINA *removes her scarf and hat and bends down to place them in
her bag.* DAVIS *shoots* MATT *a look as if to say, "What the hell are you
doing? Don't be such a geek."* MATT *quickly rises and crosses back to his
desk, sits.*

DAVIS How's the writing going?
MATT It's going.

DAVIS Matt's a playwright. I don't know how to say that in
     French. *Plum de drama* or whatever.
MATT *Le dramatiste.* (*To* CHRISTINA.) Is that right—*le dramatiste*?
CHRISTINA Yes. *Le dramatiste. L'auteur.*
DAVIS Christina's from Paris. She's been in Amsterdam for how
     long now—five years?

CHRISTINA *holds up three fingers.*

DAVIS *Trois*, right. Before that she lived in the Latin Quarter and
     worked at one of those Australian bars. (*To* CHRISTINA.) Matt
     and I were freshman roommates in university. (*To* MATT.)
     Christina's a singer.
MATT Cool. What kind of stuff do you sing?
CHRISTINA Nina Simone. Sara Vaughan. Billie Holiday. Judy
     Garland.
DAVIS Back in Paris she had a weekly cabaret gig at some bar
     called—what was it called again?
CHRISTINA Polly Magoo's.
DAVIS Say it again.
CHRISTINA Polly Magoo's.
DAVIS Say it again.
CHRISTINA Polly Magoo's.
DAVIS (*under his breath*) Oh, my god—
MATT I know it.
DAVIS You do?
MATT Last week we walked past it like four times.
DAVIS No shit?
MATT Yeah, we actually went in for a minute but you wouldn't
     stay because you said it looked seedy. Dark floorboards.
     Ancient wooden booths. Old lady with bad teeth
     behind the bar.

DAVIS Right. Polly Wants a Crackpipe Magoo's. Where they
    scowl at you if you're over five-foot-six and exhibit even the
    slightest modicum of North American decency.

DAVIS *stands suddenly.* MATT *stands as well.*

DAVIS *Excuse moi* [*substitute a smattering of bad faux French*] . . .
    faire pipi.

DAVIS *exits to the bathroom, closes the door.* MATT *sits.*

MATT *and* CHRISTINA *sit in silence. There is some fraternity
party–like shouting from another hostel room.*

MATT It's weird how everyone here sounds like they're from
    Madison, Wisconsin . . . You must meet a lot of annoying
    Americans. I mean, we blow into town, smoke all your pot,
    drink all your Heineken . . . You must get like, *"Merde!
    Beaucoup des frat boys! Courons aux montaigne . . ."*

CHRISTINA *touches the coffee stain on her sweater, and then removes
her hat and then her sweater. Bare-breasted now, she reaches into her
purse, produces a V-neck T-shirt and some deodorant.* MATT *turns away
during the nudity. She applies the deodorant, slips into the new shirt,
stuffs the sweater in her bag.*

CHRISTINA May I have a cigarette?
MATT You may, but no. I mean I don't . . . I'm sort of a part-time
    smoker. I ran out. But Davis'll have some. He bought a carton
    of Camel Lights at the duty-free at KFC—I mean JFK. Soft
    packs, I think they were.

An awkward pause.

MATT So you're um really pretty.
CHRISTINA Thank you.
MATT Sure. No problem.

The sound of the toilet flushing. DAVIS *returns from the bathroom with one of his signature kung-fu entrances. He is now holding a large, well-made café joint.*

DAVIS Shall we?

He lights the joint, smokes, passes it to CHRISTINA. *She takes a hit, passes it to* MATT.

MATT I better not.
DAVIS Oh, come on, man.
MATT No, I really shouldn't. (*To* CHRISTINA.) I'm still on these antibiotics. *Les medicaments* . . . I got like this infection thing a month and a half ago. Back in New York. This bacteria strain. In my intestines. *Les intestines.*
DAVIS Matty-boy was in pretty bad shape for a minute there.
MATT Yeah, I lost a bunch of weight. Couldn't keep anything down. It's this thing called giardia. You get it from drinking, um, fecal water. Like water that's contaminated from people's uh (*he makes a vague gesture involving his bowels*).

DAVIS *makes a farting noise like a French horn.*

MATT Well, you know . . . Usually you get it camping. I got it from this restaurant on East 4th Street.

DAVIS It's also known as "beaver fever." (*He laughs.*) Every time I hear that, I imagine fecal beavers. Like this fleet of giant beavers unloading schooner-size turds in some glacial lake. (*He laughs.*) I also imagine the beavers actually made out of feces. Like sculpted or whatever. And then, of course, there's the classic adolescent poontang thing. "Beaver Fever!"

Over the following, DAVIS *crosses to* MATT, *who is sitting on the desk now. He sits next to him and pushes* MATT *off the desk and toward* CHRISTINA. MATT *winds up sitting on the bed next to* CHRISTINA.

DAVIS Like hundreds of undergraduate males going apeshit for pussy. Like needing it so bad they affect an actual fever. Can't you just see it? Overcrowded infirmaries. Campus-wide sedation. Twenty-year-old undeclared, blue-balled males moaning into the night like cows.
CHRISTINA Cows?
DAVIS Yeah, cows. Boob milk.

DAVIS *thinks this is the funniest thing he's ever said in his life and laughs until his laughter expires.*

DAVIS Actually, when you come to think of it, the fecal beaver thing really doesn't make much sense because "fecal" and "fever" aren't exactly what you'd call smoking homonyms. (*To* CHRISTINA.) You probably have no idea what I just said.
MATT Yeah, that was pretty layered.
CHRISTINA What is "beaver"?
DAVIS God, I love Frog chicks. The accent, the intrigue.
MATT Um. A beaver is like this sort of hefty aquatic rodent with a flat tail. And buck teeth.

DAVIS Think extra-large sewer rat with a canoe oar sticking out
    of its ass.

DAVIS *imitates a buck-toothed, extra-large sewer rat with a canoe oar*
sticking out of its ass. He pulls the invisible canoe oar out of his ass and
canoes across the room doing some sort of clichéd Native American
Indian chant. He sits on the other bed, smokes the joint, and passes it to
CHRISTINA. *She takes it, smokes.*

DAVIS Smokin' in Amsterdam. Two guys and a girl. (*To* MATT.)
    Aren't Frogs cool when they smoke? I mean, we Americans
    smoke like we have glaucoma or like our fucking eyelashes are
    on fire or some shit, but Frogs, man. It's like it's an aperi*tif* or
    this preamble to sex or something.
MATT Oh, by the way, can Christina have a cigarette?
DAVIS What are you, her handler?
MATT Um. No.
DAVIS Did I miss the telekinetic interplay?
MATT She asked me for a cigarette while you were in the
    bathroom.
DAVIS But what.
MATT What.
DAVIS You said—
MATT I didn't say but.
DAVIS I know, but you wanted to. But what.
MATT Nothing.

Awkward pause.

DAVIS What, did something happen when I was in the
    bathroom?
MATT No.

DAVIS Really.

MATT Nothing happened. Forget it.

Awkward pause. Awkward glances.

DAVIS You sure nothing happened when I was in the bathroom?

MATT Davis, chill.

DAVIS Christina?

MATT Nothing fucking happened. She wanted a cigarette and I didn't have any!

DAVIS Because you don't smoke.

MATT Just drop it, okay, fucker?!

MATT *rises, crosses back to the desk, sits in the chair.* DAVIS *reaches into his pocket, removes a soft pack of Camel Lights, produces two cigarettes.*

DAVIS Would ye like a cigarette, Christina?

She nods. DAVIS *hands one to* CHRISTINA, *puts the other in his mouth so that it is paired with the joint now. He produces a lighter, lights her, lights himself, and they smoke the cigarette and the joint simultaneously.*

CHRISTINA You look like a walrus.

He smokes both again to entertain her in a walrus sort of way and then whispers something in her ear. They share a laugh.

MATT What.

DAVIS Nothing.

They laugh.

ADAM RAPP

MATT What's so funny?

DAVIS It's just you keep holding on to that belt like you're gonna . . .

MATT (*standing quickly*) Like I'm gonna what?

DAVIS I don't know. I just think Christina and I should be prepared if there's gonna be some sort of spontaneous flogging ritual.

MATT *opens the desk drawer, puts the belt in the drawer, closes it, then sits.*

DAVIS Now what were we talking about before?

MATT Um. My giardia.

DAVIS Right. Matt's giardia. Shall we continue to pursue that scatological subject matter —no pun intended wink-wink—or opt for a new theme?

MATT Where's the pun?

DAVIS What?

MATT You said no pun intended.

DAVIS I actually said no pun intended wink-wink.

MATT Right. I guess I missed the pun.

DAVIS Subject matter.

MATT I don't get it.

DAVIS Well, think about it, Herr Wunderkind, there's *subject* matter and then there's the *matter* that's been like napalming out of your *anus* for the past six weeks. Get it?

MATT I do.

DAVIS Makes sense?

MATT It does. Witty.

DAVIS IQs are skyrocketing all around.

DAVIS *rises, grabs the ashtray from the windowsill, crosses to the corner by the door, smokes for a moment.*

CHRISTINA Has your health improved?

MATT Yeah, everything's pretty much cleared up now. I mean, no more, you know . .

DAVIS Septic disasters?

MATT Right.

DAVIS Exploding green feces?

MATT Thanks, Davis.

DAVIS (*crossing back to the bed opposite* CHRISTINA *with the ashtray*) You should've seen it, Christina, it was really sort of bizarre. The violent verdant volume that this skinny fucker could produce—

MATT You're being an ass, dude.

DAVIS (*mock indignant*) What.

MATT Violent verdant volume?

DAVIS *laughs, takes another hit from the joint, passes it to* CHRISTINA.

CHRISTINA No, thank you. I am very stoned.

DAVIS Good. (*To* MATT, *looking at* CHRISTINA.) She's so pretty, isn't she, Matt?

MATT Um, very much so, actually, yes.

Suddenly the sound of distant church bells. CHRISTINA *turns and looks out the window behind her.* DAVIS *makes some silly gesture to* MATT, *somehow trying to urge* MATT *on. The bells cease and* CHRISTINA *turns her attention back to the room.*

MATT (*to* CHRISTINA) The bottom line is that I'm still finishing the antibiotics and I'm not supposed to drink or take drugs.

DAVIS Dude, I totally understand the no-drinking thing but smoking pot's not gonna like mutate with the antibiotics in some weird way. If anything, it'll probably be good for the nausea.

MATT I know, I just . . .

DAVIS You just what? The little instructions from the pharmacy say no *barbiturates* and no *alcohol*.

MATT I'd rather not risk it.

DAVIS Pot is technically a hallucinogen, right, Christina? *Le hallucinacion?*

MATT Next subject, please.

DAVIS *suddenly does a horse imitation, pulling his lips out and clucking through his teeth. He punctuates it with a titanic whinny.*

DAVIS *Les cheveux d'amour.*

MATT *Cheval.*

DAVIS *Cheval, cheveux,* what's the difference.

MATT Well, actually *cheveux* is *hair* and *cheval* is *horse.* Based on your little performance I think it's a safe bet to say that you were intending to say the *horse* of love, not the *hair* of love.

DAVIS And what if I wanted to say the *hairy* horse of love? . . . Christina, Matt can read Latin. And he can quote Robert Frost poems and the various statutes of Aristotelian Poetics. And his SAT scores were just. Off. The fucking. Charts!

MATT *shakes his head.*

CHRISTINA (*to* MATT) What is your drama about?

MATT It's actually about a young train engineer.

CHRISTINA Oh.

MATT You know what that means?

CHRISTINA Yes.

MATT Cool.

DAVIS . . . Well, tell her more.

MATT (*to* CHRISTINA) You really want to know?

CHRISTINA I am curious, yes.

DAVIS *S'il vous plait, mon canard. Mon champignon. Mon fromage—*

MATT Shut up, Davis. (*To* CHRISTINA.) It's about this rookie train engineer. On his first time out at the front of this huge freight line hauling some environmentally toxic combustible fuel, this '69 Buick Electra 225 stalls on the tracks ahead of him. He puts the train into emergency but it takes a mile and a half to stop a freight train because of all the impending megatonnage, so the young engineer can't stop in time and he hits the car, which is populated by a family of four. The Buick is severed in half and a young mother and her infant daughter who were in the backseat are killed instantly. Like blown to pollen. The father and their little boy live—the father unscratched, the boy barely makes it—and years later, through a series of letters, the train engineer, pretending to be some sort of generic representative of the railroad, anonymously contacts the father and they correspond a bit and the engineer road-trips to their home in Pittsburgh and the little boy is seven now but he's a mental vegetable from the accident and the train engineer gives the father a bunch of money that he'd been saving and the father takes it and a half a dozen or so Juenglings later—that's a local Pittsburgh beer—the engineer confesses his true identity and after an awkward moment or two they make their peace and then the train engineer asks if there's anything else he can do to help and the father asks him to kill his son. Well, to like remove his oxygen mask when he's sleeping because at night the boy forgets how to breathe sometimes because of cognitive malfunctions or whatever and he has to wear this like free-flowing Lucite oxygen mask. And the engineer does it. He removes the mask and kills the kid . . .

DAVIS Dark fucker. Tell her the title.

MATT Oh, it's called *Speckled Birds* but I'm not married to that
    yet. I might call it *Roundhouse Winter* instead. A roundhouse is
    this like donut-shaped depot where they house and switch
    locomotives . . . Did that whole thing make any sense?

CHRISTINA *nods.*

MATT I didn't speak too fast or anything?
CHRISTINA No. I understood.
MATT Cool. Sometimes I speak too fast.
DAVIS When Matt was a kid he stammered.
MATT And when Davis was a sophomore in college he got busted
    masturbating in the basement of the reference library with a
    pair of women's pantyhose noosed around his neck.
DAVIS Yeah, you like half pass out right when you start blowing
    your load. It feels pretty fucking groovy, you should try it
    sometime.

Pause.

CHRISTINA Your drama sounds very sad.
MATT It's sort of a tragedy, yeah.
DAVIS What's your hero's name again—Halifax?
MATT Hallux.
DAVIS Yeah, Hallux. How do you spell that?
MATT Um. H-a-l-l-u-x.
DAVIS *Hallux.*
MATT What, you have a problem with it?
DAVIS I don't know. "Hallux the Railroad Man." It just sounds
    made up or something.
MATT It's not made up.

DAVIS Oh. Is it an actual name?

MATT I mean, not like *Larry*, but it's a word.

DAVIS It is?

MATT Yeah.

DAVIS Huh. What's its origin?

MATT Latin.

DAVIS And it means . . . ?

MATT It means ankle.

DAVIS You sure about that?

MATT Pretty sure, yeah.

DAVIS Like sprain-your-ankle, ankle?

MATT Like the chancellor of Dickville broke his ankle sticking his foot in his mouth, yeah.

DAVIS I don't know, Matt.

MATT Well, what does it mean?

DAVIS I'm gonna go out on a limb and say big toe.

MATT Big toe.

DAVIS Yeah, big toe.

MATT Like he-stubbed-his-big-toe big toe?

DAVIS Like the mayor of Spermtown had a hard time pulling his big toe out of his recently ravaged ass, yeah.

MATT *tosses the dictionary to him.* DAVIS *catches it.*

MATT Look it up.

DAVIS Should I?

MATT Go ahead.

DAVIS I mean, I wouldn't want to humiliate you in front of Christina or anything.

MATT I'll take my chances.

DAVIS Christina, Matt's what we in the world of letters call a
    wordsmith. A lover of language. He's a bit of a pedant, too,
    but we'll talk about that at our next Cultural Enrichment
    Summit. The truth is he's a damn good playwright. Outside of
    a small, vaguely attended, weeklong showcase at this place
    called La Mama that feels more like a community center for
    recovering glue huffers than a theater, he hasn't had a single
    production, bless his heart. But he keeps plugging away. Old
    Sissyphus himself.

MATT *Sissyphus?*—

DAVIS Pushin' that rock. But there is light at the end of the old
    Hershey Highway as he recently got this award for being
    burgeoning or something. What was it called again?

MATT Why?

DAVIS *Why?*

MATT Don't.

DAVIS Don't what?

MATT Just don't.

DAVIS Come on, nerd, brag a little.

MATT (*to* CHRISTINA) He loves doing this.

DAVIS You got an award for being burgeoning. You got paid like
    ten grand. Own that shit.

MATT Own your ass, buttfucker.

DAVIS Oh, we shan't go there, shan't we.

Pause.

MATT (*to* CHRISTINA) It's called The Hayden Gray Tharp Award
    for Emerging Playwrights. (*To* DAVIS.) *Emerging*, not fucking
    burgeoning.

CHRISTINA Congratulations.

MATT Thanks.

DAVIS Matt's been emerging for so long methinks he's setting some sort of record. He's like the Olympic Gold Medalist for emerging playwrights. But we shall overcome, as they say.

Awkward pause.

CHRISTINA I very much like the title of your play. *Speckled . . . Birds?*

MATT Yeah, *Speckled Birds*. It's actually sort of a double entendre.

DAVIS (*to* CHRISTINA, *with bad French accent*) *Double entendre.*

CHRISTINA *holds up two fingers, nods.* DAVIS *holds up two fingers as well and then, when* CHRISTINA *turns her attention to* MATT, *at some point over the following,* DAVIS *performs a bit of cunnilingus between his parted fingers for* MATT*'s benefit.*

MATT You see, the um windshield of any train engine collides with a lot of birds. So there's lots of spots or speckles. *Les oiseaux pointillés.* Which doesn't totally make sense because the title would suggest that the actual birds are speckled, speckled being the descriptive qualifier, not the windshield of the train engine, but I'm not so worried about that. It's also the name of this amphetamine that railroad men take to stay awake. *Amphetamine.* Well, that's actually called speckled *bird*. It's used only in the singular.

DAVIS Why don't you just call it *Hallux,* colon space, *The Tragic Ode of a Young Everyman's First Day on the Railroad?*

MATT Why don't you close your mouth and spare us the manure slide.

DAVIS Oooh, Red Rover, Red Rover, send Matty right over.

MATT *rises very quickly, as does* DAVIS, *but* MATT *thinks better of it, or at least he pretends to for a moment.* DAVIS *gloats to* CHRISTINA *a bit and then* MATT *goes in for the kill but* DAVIS *very swiftly puts him down, with* MATT*'s arm forced up behind his back. With his other hand,* DAVIS *forces* MATT*'s head into the carpet.*

DAVIS Ooh, you damn bastard, your tiger style is no good
     here! . . . Tap out . . . Come on, tap out.

MATT *hits the floor with his hand and* DAVIS *releases him.* MATT *rises off the floor, clearly humiliated, and moves to sit in the desk chair, but* DAVIS *swipes it away and uses it like a lion tamer to force* MATT *to sit next to* CHRISTINA.

DAVIS Christina, I keep trying to get Matt here to cross back over
     into fiction, but he insists on slumming in the theatre like some
     sort of third-class peasant. In university he was a damn good
     short-story writer. He was like a young Raymond Carver.

When MATT *is properly seated,* DAVIS *puts the chair in the hallway and closes the door, then crosses to the desk, sits on it.*

MATT I can't stand Raymond Carver.
DAVIS Oh, that's right, you're one of those Henry Miller hos.
MATT Miller was a genius. Carver was all craft and no substance.
DAVIS I'm sorry but Carver could've written Miller under the
     table on any day of the week.
MATT What, like ready, set, write?
DAVIS Like pound-for-pound Carver was a better writer. Period.

MATT The biggest difference between Carver and Miller, besides Carver's obvious lack-of-style-passing-off-as-minimalism, is that Carver was a writer and Miller was an author.

DAVIS Yeah, a gob of spit and all of that. How fucking sexy.

MATT Davis, in another twenty years, they're gonna forget all about Raymond Carver and his little tales of suburban paralysis. And a *hundred* and twenty years after that, in some Parisian basement along the Seine, there will be an anticapitalist literary preservationist group binding Henry Miller bibles with thread spun from the intestines of poets. They'll be hand-sewing the spines. Knitting every signature. Each completed volume will be anointed like a sacrament. No one could juxtapose the decay and grace of our humanity better. The fury with the joy. Miller turned sewage into poetry. His language was ecstatic. You could feel the velocity with which he wrote flying across the page. Carver wrote constipated, mediocre claptrap from the kitchen table of his upstate suburban home.

DAVIS So Carver was constipated. I guess that would make Miller the literary equivalent of what—giardia?

MATT (*to* CHRISTINA) I just love how these young editors pull their first acquisition out of the slush pile and they suddenly think they're Maxwell fucking Perkins.

DAVIS Hey, that novel I pulled out of the slush pile hasn't done too badly. *You* even liked it, Mister Literary Fucking Litmus Test.

MATT I'll admit it's a good novel.

DAVIS The other day you said it was a great work of art.

MATT I did?

DAVIS I swear, Christina, the God of Frog strike me as I'm standing here. In a rare moment of artistic armistice, on the platform of the Gare du Nord, while waiting to board the train to your lovely Amsterdam, Mattyboy here turned to me and said that the novel I had acquired for my company out of the slush pile was a *great work of art*. Not a great novel, story, or composition. A great *work*. Of *art*.

MATT I just said that so you would help me pay for my train ticket.

DAVIS Oh, bullshit. You know you loved that book.

MATT It's a good novel. You did some very nice work on it, Davis. Made the dedication page and everything. I'm sure our brothers and sisters at Brown University are very proud.

MATT *suddenly rises, moves to the window, tries to open it. It doesn't budge. He tries again.*

DAVIS It won't open.

MATT *continues trying.*

DAVIS I think they actually nail them shut.

MATT *continues struggling.* DAVIS *makes he-man sounds, throws in another French-horn fart for good measure.* MATT *struggles with the window for another moment, gives up, then crosses to the door and goes out into the hallway.*

DAVIS Tune in next week, ladies and gentlemen, when our hundred-and-fifty-two-pound lactose-intolerant hero puts a Barcelona chair through the window of his hotel room. Will he free himself from the clutches of despair? Will he ever be able to escape his own noisome body odor and gastrointestinal impediments? Don't miss our next exciting episode. *Aaaaand* commercial . . .

MATT *returns with the chair, sets it at the desk, crosses back to the door, slams it, sits in the chair.*

DAVIS What about you, Christina? Who's your favorite scribe?

CHRISTINA What is scribe?

DAVIS Writer.

CHRISTINA I very much like this person Harry Potter.

DAVIS Of course you do!

CHRISTINA He is extremely smart. And boyishly handsome.

DAVIS Well, whattaya know, Frogs love Harry Potter, too! They weren't even interested in one of the most celebrated new literary American novels of last year, but they get their panties in a knot for Harry Fucking Potter. That's so, I don't know, reverse xenophobic.

MATT That doesn't even make any sense.

DAVIS Why not?

MATT Because J. K. Rowling isn't American.

DAVIS She's not?

MATT No.

DAVIS Where is she from—Nova Scotia?

MATT She's English.

DAVIS Well I say amen to Harry Fucking Potter! And I'd say it in Frog if I knew how to say it.

MATT *Tu es un poisson salopé.*

CHRISTINA *laughs.*

DAVIS What does that mean?

MATT Nothing. What you said. About Harry Potter.

CHRISTINA *laughs some more, then covers her mouth.*

DAVIS You ever read Henry Miller, Christina?

CHRISTINA Yes.

DAVIS In Frog or American?

CHRISTINA In English. He is very popular in Paris.

DAVIS Which one did you read?

CHRISTINA *Tropic of Cancer.*

DAVIS You like it?

CHRISTINA I liked it very much, yes.

DAVIS You ever read any Raymond Carver?

CHRISTINA I do not know this person.

MATT (*standing*) My point, exactly. The rest of the world thinks
he's provincial.

DAVIS *stares at* MATT *until he sits back in the chair.* CHRISTINA *rises,
shoulders her purse.* MATT *and* DAVIS *rise as well.*

CHRISTINA Please excuse me for a moment.

CHRISTINA *exits to the bathroom with her purse.* MATT *crosses to his
bed, pretends to adjust the pillow.*

DAVIS So what do you think?

MATT About what?

DAVIS About Christina.

MATT She's nice.

DAVIS That's it—she's nice?

MATT I like her.

DAVIS She's fucking beautiful, bro.

MATT Yeah, she's pretty.

DAVIS A hundred and fifty fucking oyros pretty.

MATT *Oyros?* What is that, like *Funyuns?*

DAVIS You're still up for this, right?

MATT Sure.

DAVIS *Sure?*

MATT Yeah, it's cool.

DAVIS You don't sound too excited.

MATT No, I just . . .

DAVIS What?

MATT *sits on the bed, starts to cry.*

DAVIS Oh, no, don't start this shit again.

MATT *cries.*

DAVIS Fuck.

DAVIS *crosses to* MATT *on the bed, hugs him, attempts to give comfort.*
MATT *holds on for dear life, calms down after a moment.*

DAVIS You okay?

MATT *nods, still getting it together.* DAVIS *sits next to him.*

DAVIS Look, Matt, you need this.

MATT *nods, struggles for a moment.*

DAVIS You sure you're okay?

MATT Yes.

DAVIS Because she's not gonna want to even *touch* you if you're
    blubbering all over yourself. Frog chicks don't like that.

MATT Stop calling her a Frog.

DAVIS She knows I'm kidding. She likes it.

MATT *almost loses it again.*

DAVIS If you start crying again I'm gonna kick your ass.
     You're thirty years old and you're gonna fucking do
     this. So stop feeling sorry for yourself and get your shit
     together.

MATT *gets himself together, grabs the dictionary, crosses to the desk
with it, starts to arrange his pens and things.*

DAVIS By the way, she shaves her pussy.

MATT She does?

DAVIS Clean as a car seat.

MATT How do you know?

DAVIS Because I know. She showed it to me.

MATT Why?

DAVIS It's what they do. To assure the clientele that they don't
     have venereal warts or yeast or whatever.

MATT Did you mess around?

DAVIS We made out.

MATT You made out?

DAVIS Yeah. So what?

MATT Jesus, Davis.

DAVIS Jesus what?

MATT Nothing. I just . . . forget it.

MATT *crosses to his shelf, removes his toiletries, and starts to place them
in his traveling bag, which is under his bed.*

DAVIS I had to earn her trust. She wouldn't come back with me unless I proved that I didn't have dubious intentions.

From his travel bag, MATT *removes a moth-eaten cardigan sweater and puts it on. He then removes his shoes, and uses the cylinder of musk spray that* DAVIS *had used at the top of the act to deodorize his socked feet.*

MATT So you like *made out* made out?

DAVIS Yeah, we French kissed. With tongue and such. I felt her up a little, too.

MATT Like her tits?

DAVIS Yeah, her tits.

MATT Are you gonna tell Sarah?

DAVIS This has nothing to do with Sarah. Why, are you?

MATT Of course not. But—

DAVIS But what?

MATT Well, you're sort of like engaged.

DAVIS What, are you judging me?

MATT No.

DAVIS Good. Because that would suck. Ye holy disciple of Henry Miller.

MATT I'm not judging you.

DAVIS Just remember, let him that casts the first stone . . .

MATT *puts his shoes back on, ties them.*

MATT So she shaves it?

DAVIS She does indeed, my skinny white brother.

MATT And you like that?

DAVIS I do, yeah. It's like a cold cut or something.

MATT *shoves his travel bag back under the bed, crosses to the door, almost opens it to check the hall, thinks better of it.*

MATT So you made out with her and felt her up where—in like one of those display windows?

DAVIS Pretty much. I mean she closed the curtain.

MATT It sounds like some oversized terrarium.

DAVIS It was a little room. Shag carpeting. Queen-sized bed. Mirror ball hanging from the ceiling. Little space heater off to the left. Portable cassette player resting on the headboard.

MATT Music?

DAVIS She played Waits.

MATT *Bone Machine?*

DAVIS *Small Change.*

MATT Good album.

DAVIS It's a great fucking album and she's a great fucking girl. She was the best-looking one in all the windows.

MATT *walks over to the shelf over the bed, turns off the small lamp.*

MATT So what—you just like walked up to her?

DAVIS She called me over.

MATT Like over a PA?

DAVIS No, she beckoned me.

MATT How?

DAVIS She waved.

DAVIS *demonstrates the wave.*

MATT Wow.

DAVIS I know, right?

MATT That would be cool.

DAVIS It was totally cool. I mean, I got the feeling that she really wanted me. Don't get me wrong, I know there's like hundreds of people every day who she probably suckers like that but I really felt singled out. And that's how it'll be for you, too. She'll make you feel special . . . Just think of those legs wrapped around you.

DAVIS *uses* CHRISTINA*'s coat to demonstrate and has a little fun miming sex with her.*

MATT Does she like um know—

DAVIS Why she's here? Of course she does. We talked about it.

MATT She probably thinks I'm some sort of freak.

DAVIS I just told her you were shy. Frog chicks dig shy. She likes you, I can tell.

MATT You really think so?

DAVIS You should see the way she was looking at you.

MATT When?

DAVIS When you were talking about your play. And during that load of shit about Henry Miller. She was all over it.

MATT Really?

DAVIS I swear.

MATT So what, you'll like leave?

DAVIS Yeah, I'll leave. She'll be all yours.

DAVIS *hands* CHRISTINA*'s coat to Matt. He holds it for a moment and then hangs it on one of the three coat hooks on the upstage wall.*

MATT Where will you go?

DAVIS I'll go to Café Space Cake, eat a flooginflaffin. Gaze at the architecture.

MATT *thinks a moment.*

MATT Was she . . . ?
DAVIS What, a good kisser?
MATT Yeah.
DAVIS She's fucking solid, bro. I mean, I didn't see fireworks
or anything, but she's legit. And her body's killer.
Dominant legs. Perfect tits. Heart-shaped ass. No weird
moles or anything. She tried jerking me off, too, but I couldn't
get it up.
MATT So she um felt you up, too?
DAVIS A little, yeah.
MATT Why couldn't you get it up?
DAVIS I don't know. I think it was the combination of all
the shrooming and the idea of *you* being with her. I sort
of wanted her to be—I don't know—*fresh* for you or
something.

MATT *quickly crosses to his laptop, seizes it, crosses to the bed, reaches
under it, removes a computer travel bag, puts the computer in it, shoves
the bag back under the bed.*

DAVIS And besides, she wanted to put this like three-ply,
industrial-strength condom on me. It would've been like
getting a massage in a snowmobile suit. But she's feral, bro.
MATT Really?
DAVIS Yeah. As in ferocious. I mean, I felt bad. She really wanted
me to get off. After I pulled the plug she felt so guilty she
actually tried to give me my money back.

MATT *rises, starts pacing, periodically picking a piece of lint or two off
the floor.*

RED LIGHT WINTER   35

MATT You didn't take it, did you?

DAVIS Of course not. I let her teabag my nuts for a few minutes, though. She felt better after that.

MATT (*stopping dead in his tracks*) She teabagged your nuts?!

DAVIS That actually felt great. But it was also [*insert ridiculous faux French word*]. Because, like I said, I was sort of preparing to give her to you. So in some weird way it was like *you* were teabagging my nuts.

MATT *stands, paces again, starts clicking his pen.*

MATT So she's pretty into this stuff?

DAVIS She's a fucking pro. But not insensitive. She really understands the value of a job well done. Oh, and while she was—

MATT Teabagging your nuts?

DAVIS Yeah, exactly, while she was teabagging my nuts she started meowing.

MATT Come on.

DAVIS I swear to you, Matt, she meowed.

MATT Like a cat?

DAVIS No, like a fucking hammerhead shark. Of course like a cat.

MATT Wow.

DAVIS See?

MATT That's weird.

DAVIS Yeah.

MATT But in a good way.

DAVIS In a totally good way.

MATT She really is pretty.

DAVIS Stop pacing. You're gonna throw your back out or something.

MATT *stops pacing.*

DAVIS And jettison that pen, man.

MATT *stops clicking his pen, places it on the desk.*

DAVIS *(proffering the joint)* You sure you don't want a hit of this?
    It's incredible.

MATT *shakes his head, starts to fix his hair.* DAVIS *rises off the bed,
crosses to the door.*

DAVIS What the fuck is she doing in there, retiling?

MATT *starts to tuck his sweater into his pants.* DAVIS *crosses to
him, untucks* MATT's *sweater, removes it, and untucks his thermal
undershirt and T-shirt and hangs the sweater on one of the three coat
hooks on the upstage wall.*

DAVIS So here's the plan: I'll stick around for a few more
    minutes, just to make sure everything's on the up-and-up,
    and at the appropriate moment I'll make a graceful exit
    and leave you two alone . . . So everything's cool, right?
MATT Yeah, everything's cool. You got any gum? ·
DAVIS No, why? Your breath stinks?
MATT My mouth tastes funny.
DAVIS Breathe on me.
MATT Why?
DAVIS Just breathe on me.
MATT No, that's weird.
DAVIS Come on, I'll tell you if you have bad breath.

DAVIS *leans into* MATT. MATT *hesitates, breathes on him.*

DAVIS You're fine.

MATT Are you sure?

DAVIS Yeah, just make sure to brush your teeth before the fireworks begin.

MATT *bolts for his bag, removes a tube of toothpaste just as* CHRISTINA *enters.* DAVIS *nudges him, urges him to stand, then sit, then stand, then sit.* CHRISTINA *turns to them after she closes the door. She is now wearing a long red dress, and her hair is up. She is also wearing nice earrings and heels. She looks beautiful.* MATT *and* DAVIS *sit,* MATT *still holding the toothpaste but not realizing it.*

DAVIS Whoa.

MATT Wow.

DAVIS We were wondering what was taking you so long.

CHRISTINA If you will allow me, I would like to sing a song.

DAVIS Like a *song* song?

CHRISTINA Yes. (*To* MATT.) Would that be okay?

MATT Totally. Yeah. It'd be great.

CHRISTINA Okay. Picture blue light and a piano.

CHRISTINA *closes her eyes. After a moment she opens her eyes, begins to sing. She sings beautifully. She is mesmerizing.*

CHRISTINA (*singing*)
In the time that it shall take
to move your body

In the time that it shall take
to lure you home

I'll find a willow tree and sleep beneath
its branches

And in its bark I'll carve my heart's
most private poem

Thirty years shall I require
to pick the lemons

Thirty more to draw the flowers
from the grove

A drop of vodka from the soil
of ancient Russia

A pinch of sea salt from the shores
of our lost cove

It's a long way to the bottom
of the ocean

The lonely mermaid braids a starfish
through her hair

Her sailor drowned twelve years ago
near Zaragosa

And counting oysters never soothed
her slow despair

It's the pearl that I long for
the pearl that I long for
the pearl that I long
to hold near

It's the pearl that I long for
the pearl that I long for

the pearl that I long for
my dear

CHRISTINA *remains suspended in the song for a moment, then comes out of it. An awkward silence. Then:*

DAVIS That fucking rocked!

CHRISTINA Thank you.

DAVIS Whose tune is that?

CHRISTINA It's one of mine.

DAVIS *You* wrote that?

CHRISTINA I composed it on the piano at Polly Magoo's.

DAVIS I say we call up Interscope, get her a record contract, right, Matt?

MATT It's a beautiful song, Christina.

CHRISTINA I am very pleased that you liked it.

DAVIS Great stuff. I mean, I have no idea what it's about as the imagery jumps around and the themes start to blur a bit but I really dig it.

CHRISTINA It's about unrequiet . . .

MATT Unrequited love?

CHRISTINA Unrequited love, yes.

DAVIS Huh. That's funny, I didn't get that.

CHRISTINA I'm sorry.

DAVIS No, don't be. Just maybe add a line or two to underscore your subject matter. I'm a firm believer in organizing the information for your audience so they're like *in* on it. I mean, Rome wasn't built in a day-care center.

Awkward pause.

MATT Did you write that in English?

CHRISTINA I did, yes.

MATT Because the lyrics are really cool.

DAVIS Yeah, the lyrics, the phrasing, the imagery!

CHRISTINA Thank you.

MATT I especially liked the deep-sea stuff: the mermaid and the oysters and all that. Going from this sort of spinal love tree to the bottom of the ocean. It's a pretty cool journey.

DAVIS Phantasmagoric.

MATT Yeah, totally surreal. And the rhyme scheme is cool too. Home and poem. And um hair and despair. And that off-rhyme coupling of ocean and Zaragosa. Really subtle but affecting. And your voice.

DAVIS Yeah, what a voice! It's like Paula Abdul meets Coretta Scott King or some shit.

MATT You have a really beautiful voice.

CHRISTINA Thank you.

Another awkward pause. CHRISTINA *remains standing.*

DAVIS (*standing suddenly, going for his coat*) Well, boys and girls, this bad little camper is gonna go hunting for a few hours of quote-unquote Amsterdamage.

MATT *stands.* DAVIS *removes a pack of Camel Lights and his Zippo lighter and sets them on the desk.*

DAVIS Let her have as many of these as she'd like.

DAVIS *gathers his coat, crosses to* CHRISTINA. *He goes to a knee, takes her hand, kisses it, chastely.*

DAVIS Madame. (*Rising.*) It was very nice to meet you, Christina.
  Enjoy the rest of your evening.

DAVIS *starts for the door.*

CHRISTINA Davis.

*He stops, turns. They face each other for a moment. Things get sort
of awkward.*

DAVIS Oh, fuck me. Did I forget to pay you?
CHRISTINA No, you paid.
DAVIS You want American dollars instead of oyros?
CHRISTINA No. I was wondering if I could have your address
  in New York.
DAVIS Why, are you gonna like invoice me for add-ons?
CHRISTINA I'd like to send you something.
DAVIS Oh. What.
CHRISTINA My music. I have a CD. From Paris.
DAVIS Cool. Sure thing.

DAVIS *crosses to the desk, grabs* MATT*'s notebook, tears out a clean
sheet, writes the address on it with* MATT*'s pen, folds the paper in half.
Before he turns back he spots the dictionary, opens it up, fingers to a spot.*

DAVIS Hallux. It's a noun and it reads and I quote: The inner
  or first digit on the hind foot of a mammal; in man, the
  big toe . . .

DAVIS *closes the dictionary, sets it back on the desk, crosses to*
MATT, *reaches into his pocket, removes a condom packet, places it
in* MATT*'s hand.*

DAVIS Lambskin.

DAVIS *then crosses to* CHRISTINA, *hands her the piece of paper. She takes it, and he kisses her on either cheek and she hugs him goodbye, holding on a little too long.* DAVIS *pats her on the back and breaks from the hug.*

DAVIS *Bon suar*, then.
CHRISTINA Goodbye.

DAVIS *exits. The door closes.* CHRISTINA *stands there for a moment, somehow paralyzed. She then crosses to the upstage bed, sits, and starts to cry.*

MATT *watches her for a moment, tries to move toward her, hesitates, then opens the door and exits to the bathroom. The sound of a tap running.* MATT *returns with a plastic cup of water, hands it to her. She drinks.*

CHRISTINA I feel so stupid.
MATT Don't.
CHRISTINA That was humiliating.
MATT What, your song? No, it was really beautiful. I'm serious.

He crosses to the cigarette pack and Zippo lighter, gets a cigarette, crosses back to her, gives her a cigarette, lights it. She smokes. He crosses to the desk, sits in the chair.

CHRISTINA When he came to visit me he was so nice. And just now he was so . . .
MATT Asshole-ish?
CHRISTINA Yes. When we were together he was so gentle.
MATT Yeah, Davis told me you guys fooled around a little.
CHRISTINA Yes.

MATT Like what did you do? If you don't mind me asking.

CHRISTINA We made love.

MATT Oh. You made love.

CHRISTINA Yes. Is that bad?

MATT No, it's just um, well, weird.

CHRISTINA Why?

MATT Oh, no reason. I mean—How many times, if you don't mind me asking?

CHRISTINA Three times.

MATT He paid for three times?

CHRISTINA He only paid for one, but I could not bring him to orgasm so I gave him two more sessions for free.

MATT Oh. So can I like ask a question?

CHRISTINA Of course.

MATT I know this isn't a court of law or anything, and it's probably none of my business, but if he didn't come, how did you like um *demarcate* each session?

CHRISTINA What is de*mar* . . .

MATT Demarcate. How did you distinguish or like measure it?

CHRISTINA Because *I* orgasm.

MATT Three times?

CHRISTINA Yes.

MATT It must have been pretty special.

CHRISTINA It was strange. We got very close. We talked. We told each other things.

MATT Like what?

CHRISTINA Personal things. About my life. About his life. About his sadness.

MATT His *sadness*?

CHRISTINA Yes. Davis possesses very much melancholy. He talked about his mother. The treatments and the cancer.

MATT His mother, the treatments, the cancer. Really.

CHRISTINA Yes.

She looks for the ashtray. It's on the other bed. MATT *crosses to it and hands it to her, crosses downstage right.*

MATT So let me get this straight. You guys quote-unquote *made love* three times.

CHRISTINA I wanted four but he wouldn't stop talking about you.

MATT What did he say?

CHRISTINA How important you are to him. And how he felt strange making love because he wanted to introduce me to you. He cares about you very much.

MATT Oh, no doubt . . . So are you like all smitten with him or something?

CHRISTINA What is smitten?

MATT Love. Are you in love with him?

CHRISTINA I don't know. Just now when he was leaving I suddenly felt like I would never see him again and it made me feel very sad.

MATT Well you probably won't . . . See him again, I mean.

CHRISTINA *turns away, smokes for a moment.* MATT *crosses back to the desk.*

MATT Christina, as a human being or whatever, I feel I should say something. And this isn't intended to burst your bubble, or like cockblock him because he really is like a brother to me, but Davis's mother is alive and well. She actually teaches comparative literature at Brandeis.

And regarding his melancholy, the only angstrom of quote-unquote *sadness* that I've ever been privy to was the time when he cried because he wasn't named a Rhodes scholar.

CHRISTINA *puts her cigarette out and reaches into her bag and removes a small snow globe of the New York City skyline. She shakes it and watches it snow for a moment.*

MATT What's that?

She hands it to him.

MATT Did Davis give you this?
CHRISTINA It's beautiful.
MATT Yeah, he bought this at a gift shop near the train station in Paris.
CHRISTINA I was very moved to receive it.
MATT I'm sure.
CHRISTINA I wish to someday go to New York.
MATT Well, you should come visit.

He hands the snow globe back to her. She stares at it for a moment, then puts it in her bag.

MATT So regarding this whole thing, we don't have to like um *do* anything if you don't want to. I mean you seemed pretty upset there and I wouldn't want you to feel like obligat—
CHRISTINA It's okay. I would like to be with you.
MATT Really? I mean, I can't guarantee you like orgasming in triplicate.
CHRISTINA That's not important.

Awkward pause.

MATT More water?

CHRISTINA No, thank you.

MATT Another cigarette?

She nods. He gives her another cigarette, lights her, then sits on the other bed.

MATT So before we continue, I have to say something. And I
might be totally off base here.

CHRISTINA What.

MATT You're not French, are you? I mean you might be, right?
But I'm almost totally sure that you're like this very talented
imposter. So you can like stop the routine. I won't tell
anybody. I mean your accent is spot-on perfect, and the slight
lack of knowledge of English vocabulary is very subtle and
authentic, i.e., your purported ignorance of words like
smitten and *demarcate* and um *scribe*, but you sort of blew it
when you sang. I mean, you have this totally like mellifluous
voice or whatever, and your song really is affecting—it's
just that there was a moment or two there where you
suddenly sounded really Midwestern. I'm from Illinois so
I have these like Des Plaines River Valley superpowers . . . I
mean, if you want to continue in like character or whatever
it's fine with me.

Suddenly a cell phone starts ringing. CHRISTINA *goes into her bag,
removes it, stands and faces the corner for privacy, answers.*

CHRISTINA Hello? *Oui . . . Oui . . . Oui . . .* No . . . No . . .

She hangs up.

MATT Who was that?

She turns to face him.

CHRISTINA *(dropping the accent, American English now)* Albert.

MATT Your boyfriend?
CHRISTINA My husband.
MATT You're married?
CHRISTINA It was arranged. He's gay, lives in Paris.

MATT *offers her the upstage bed to sit on. She hesitates, but gathers her things and does so. He crosses to the desk, leans against it over the following:*

MATT Did you like get paid a lot of money to marry him?
CHRISTINA Enough to buy an apartment here. He has dual citizenship.
MATT How often do you see him?
CHRISTINA We spend about six months out of the year together. Go to art openings. Fancy dinners. Cocktail parties. We hold hands and rub noses, put on a show for his colleagues.
MATT What does he do?
CHRISTINA He's a lawyer.
MATT You met in Paris?
CHRISTINA I was performing at this bar. After my set he sent me a note. He was hot. Dressed well. Smoked Nat Shermans. We started hanging out. It was weird, I totally thought he was straight. But we never slept together. A few weeks later he

made the offer. His lover stopped by at the end of the meeting, and we shook hands. It was all business.

MATT What if you . . .

CHRISTINA What if I what.

MATT I don't know. Like meet someone.

CHRISTINA I meet people every day.

MATT No, but I mean like what if you meet someone and . . . well, you know . . . Like what happened with Davis.

CHRISTINA It doesn't happen.

MATT Right.

She smokes. He moves the chair closer to her, sits.

MATT So where are you from, anyway?

CHRISTINA Baltimore.

MATT Oh, I would've guessed like Green Bay or something.

CHRISTINA My parents are from Madison. We moved to the East Coast when I was seven.

MATT So why the facade?

CHRISTINA I don't know. It's easier somehow.

MATT For your job?

CHRISTINA It's just easier.

MATT So this is pretty weird.

CHRISTINA Why?

MATT I don't know. You were doing this whole character thing. Mysterious French ingenue. It's like you just came out of the stage door and you're suddenly sort of normal.

She stands.

CHRISTINA If you want me to go I'll go.

He stands.

MATT No, stay.

She sits. He sits.

MATT So how did you wind up in Paris?

CHRISTINA I was in school. I did a semester abroad and never came back.

MATT What were you studying?

CHRISTINA Theater.

MATT So you're an actress.

CHRISTINA I was, yes.

MATT Where'd you go to school?

CHRISTINA Bard.

MATT What year did you go abroad?

CHRISTINA I was a sophomore.

MATT Wow. You were young . . . What was the last play you did?

CHRISTINA Fucking *Oklahoma*. But it was pretty experimental. It was set in a small engine-repair shop and all the townspeople were part machine.

They share laughter.

CHRISTINA So Davis works in book publishing?

MATT Yeah, he's recently become this like hotshit editor. He pulled this book out of the slush pile. A total random discovery. It was named a New York Times Notable Book and got all these rave reviews. Davis got promoted pretty quick after that and now he's on this fast track. He'll probably have his own imprint before he turns thirty-five. (*Standing.*) If you want me to go find him I totally will. He's probably over at that café with the foosball tables. At school he used to play people for money. He'd even take 'em on two-on-one. And he's a helluva dart player, too. The guy has the genes from some like super race. And he has this great apartment in the Village. Brick walls. East-west exposure. Flower pots on the window ledges. A Bowflex. I'll seriously go get him if you want me to.

CHRISTINA Stop acting like him. You were doing better as yourself.

MATT Right.

He sits.

CHRISTINA So Davis told me it's been a while since you've been with anyone.

MATT Yeah, it's been a while.

CHRISTINA How long?

MATT Um, like three years. Three and a half, actually.

CHRISTINA Why?

MATT I don't know. I was sort of in love with this girl. We were living together. She met some guy. Moved out. I took it pretty hard. Depression set in. I stopped doing my laundry. Drank a lot of Robitussin. Got addicted to online bridge. I guess I sort of lost my confidence after that. Davis would set me up with people. Nothing really ever felt right. For a while he actually thought I might be gay.

CHRISTINA Are you?

MATT What, gay? No way. I mean, at least I don't think I am.

CHRISTINA Have you ever been with a man?

MATT Well, in high school I had this huge crush on the captain of the football team.

CHRISTINA Really?

MATT That was a joke.

CHRISTINA Maybe you should explore it.

MATT No, I prefer women. Like I'm looking at you right now and I'm totally like balls-to-the-wall attracted to you . . .

CHRISTINA But?

MATT There's no but, really. I just sort of . . . I don't know what it is.

CHRISTINA Can you get an erection?

MATT What?

CHRISTINA Are you impotent.

MATT A perfectly legitimate question, Christina, but check it out, I get these like totally ferocious morning boners every day.

CHRISTINA What was her name?

MATT Who, the girl I was in . . . her name was Sarah. We dated for like two and a half years. Lived together for a few months. And then things got weird.

CHRISTINA How did things get weird?

MATT I don't know. They just did . . . If you want to know the truth, she sort of fell in love with Davis. And now they're together, actually. It was pretty fucked up for a while, but it's cool, now.

CHRISTINA Are you still in love with her?

MATT Who, Sarah? No. No way. She's a fucking cunt.

CHRISTINA Are they in love?

MATT Um. Yeah. They are. They're sort of perfect for each other. Davis actually bought that snow globe for her. Because of the skyline. It's the new, like post-September-eleventh version.

CHRISTINA *stands and turns away.*

MATT That's when Sarah and I split up and she and Davis, well, got together. It's really hard to find new skyline stuff in New

York. I mean they have key chains and like T-shirts and stuff, but they all have images of the Twin Towers or bands of light where they would be still standing or whatever.

CHRISTINA *turns to him.*

MATT He's not who you think he is, Christina. Whatever happened between you two. It wasn't real. I know that probably sucks to hear . . .
CHRISTINA So how many women have you been with?
MATT Well, not many, actually.
CHRISTINA Are you a virgin?
MATT No. I mean, it's a staggeringly low number of women. Like two, if truth be told.
CHRISTINA Who were they?
MATT Well, I was with Sarah. A lot. Like every day.

CHRISTINA *crosses to the upstage bed, sits.*

MATT And I was with this other girl back in college who liked this haiku I wrote about a pair of pajamas.
CHRISTINA Come here.
MATT What do you mean?
CHRISTINA I mean come here. Sit next to me.
MATT Like join you on the bed?
CHRISTINA Yeah.

MATT *hesitates, rises, sets the chair in front of the desk, crosses to her at the bed, sits. He starts bobbing up and down a bit.*

MATT The beds here are pretty firm. Good for bouncing . . .
CHRISTINA Kiss me.

He stops bobbing.

MATT Are you sure?

CHRISTINA Yeah.

MATT Do you really want me to, or is this like some sort of pity-the-nerd exercise?

She pulls him into her. They kiss for a moment. They stop.

MATT Was that okay?

CHRISTINA It was nice.

MATT Is my breath . . . I mean, I could—

CHRISTINA Your breath is perfect.

MATT Oh, cool.

He folds into himself.

MATT So, can I kiss you again?

CHRISTINA Do you want to?

MATT I do, yeah.

CHRISTINA So do it.

He leans into her and they kiss again. It lasts a little longer. When it ends, CHRISTINA *stands, starts to take her dress off.*

MATT That's a great dress.

CHRISTINA Thanks.

MATT Really, really great. Very um flattering, etcetera, etcetera.

CHRISTINA The zipper gets caught at the top. Will you help me undo it?

ADAM RAPP

MATT Sure.

He stands, takes a step toward her, reaches toward the zipper, stops, closes his eyes.

MATT Um, I think I should say some things.
CHRISTINA What.
MATT I'm an insomniac . . . I haven't slept in over six weeks . . .
    And I was going to kill myself tonight.
CHRISTINA Open your eyes.

MATT *opens his eyes.*

CHRISTINA Why?
MATT I don't know. I was just sitting there. In that chair and . . . I
    just wanted everything to stop . . . I used my belt. I actually
    had it rigged to a hook on the wall and I had started to um . . .
    hang myself . . . when you guys came in . . . And now I'm glad
    I didn't do it . . . I just needed to say that, Christina. I'm glad
    you came in.

*They look at each other for a long moment and then she turns around
again. He moves to her, unzips the dress. She crosses to the light, turns it
out. Only the light from the window now. She lets her hair down, steps
out of the dress. She stands naked before him for a moment, then helps
him undress, removing his shoes, his shirt, his pants, his socks, until he
is naked too. She then takes his hand and leads him to the bed. They
sit before each other and* MATT *draws the covers over his shoulders. She
licks her hand and then masturbates him for a moment. She removes the
condom from the packet and puts it on his erect penis. He touches her
face and she pulls him on top of her. They kiss for a moment and then he*

inserts his penis and they start to slowly make love. It quickly picks up speed. It is brief but something real passes between them. After MATT comes, he collapses on top of her, and falls instantly asleep. CHRISTINA stares out for a moment, and then pushes him off of her, gets out of bed, and dresses at the foot of the other bed.

She gathers her things and crosses to where her dress fell to the floor. She picks it up, considers it, and then crosses to the chair and lays it across the arms of the chair. She then reaches into her bag and removes a small portable cassette player. She sets it on the desk, watches MATT sleep for a moment. She grabs DAVIS's cigarettes and lighter that were left on the desk, puts them in her bag, and quietly exits, closing the door behind her.

After a moment, MATT wakes as if he was dreaming that he was falling. He sits up in bed, disoriented. He looks around, then reaches down, removes the condom, places it on the windowsill. He gets out of bed, crosses to the door, opens it, looks out into the hallway. He then sees the dress laid over the arms of the chair. He takes it, pulls it into him, holds it for a moment. He then spots the cassette player, presses Play. Tom Waits's "Tom Traubert's Blues" plays. He sits holding the dress as lights fade to black.

ACT II

A year later.

Dusk.

MATT's *small nine-by-twelve-foot domicile in the East Village. A twin bed, up against one wall. The bed is made. On the floor beside the bed, several stacks of books as well as a few stray items of clothing that never found their way to the laundry bag. A small kitchenette with a half-fridge, a short countertop, a single cupboard, a portable stove top, a sink, and other space-saving items. Above the sink, a window facing an airshaft. Against one wall, over the twin bed, a homemade library fashioned from planks of wood, a phone–slash–answering machine unit on the bottom shelf. A few pictures and postcards of literary titans arranged on the wall: Henry Miller, John Fante, Jim Carroll, Frederick Exley, Arthur Miller, Bertolt Brecht, and Raymond Carver. In black Sharpie ink, there is a large X scrawled over Carver's face. Next to the bed, a slightly cluttered desk containing a few paperback novels, a dictionary, a bottle of sleeping pills, a laptop computer, a cheap manual-feed printer, a few bottles of various liquid antihistamines, a Kleenex box, and the portable cassette player from the end of Act I. Between the desk and the bed is a closet, whose door is closed. Downstage of the desk is an electric space heater. The room is generally neat, but the enormous volume of books gives it a congested, almost claustrophobic quality.*

MATT *is seated at the desk. He is dressed in corduroy pants, a thick sweater, and wool socks. There is an afghan throw draped over his shoulders. He is writing. After a moment, he stops and checks the space*

heater, fidgets a bit, blows into cupped hands, returns to his computer.
He writes for a bit and then stops again. He looks out the window, rises
off the chair, goes for the Kleenex box, sees that it is empty, exits the
room, and returns moments later with a wad of toilet paper that he uses
to clean the dust off his computer screen. He presses a button on the
portable cassette player. "Jitterbug Boy" from Tom Waits's Small Change
plays. He listens for a moment and then presses Stop, rewinds it, listens
again. He does this twice, then sits there, blank. He reaches for the
sleeping pills, undoes the top, fingers into the bottle, and removes two
pills, arranges them next to each other on his desk. A knock at the door.
MATT *quickly stops the cassette player, freezes. Another knock.* MATT
puts the pills back in the bottle, sits very still. A WOMAN'S VOICE *calls*
out from the other side of the door.

VOICE Hello?

MATT *doesn't respond.*

VOICE Davis, is that you?
MATT No. Davis isn't here.
VOICE Oh. Are you sure?
MATT Yeah, I'm positive.
VOICE Are you one of his roommates or something?
MATT Um. No.
VOICE I'm sorry to bother you but I was led to believe that Davis
    lives here.
MATT He doesn't.
VOICE Well this is the address he gave me.
MATT He's never lived here.
VOICE But you know him, right?

MATT *doesn't answer, rewinds the cassette player.*

VOICE I said you know him, right?

MATT I do, yeah.

VOICE Well, can you tell me where I might be able to find him?

MATT Who are you?

VOICE A friend.

MATT (*standing*) A friend from where?

VOICE I met him last winter. I'm just passing through town and I
    was hoping to say hello.

MATT Did he know you were coming?

VOICE No. I wanted to surprise him.

MATT How did you get in the building?

VOICE The front door was open. Is he in there or something? . . .
    Hello?

MATT Yeah.

VOICE Did you hear me?

MATT I heard you. He's not here.

VOICE Do you know where I might be able to find him?

MATT I'm not sure. I mean it's Saturday night. Most people
    have plans.

VOICE It doesn't seem like *you* have any plans.

MATT What?

VOICE I said it doesn't seem like you have any plans.

MATT I'm working.

VOICE On what?

MATT Nothing. I'm just working.

VOICE Mysterious . . . Mysterious work being done behind a
    mysterious door.

MATT Look, if you want to leave Davis a message I'll be sure he
    gets it the next time I see him.

VOICE Can I maybe get his phone number?

MATT I'm not sure that's such a good idea.

VOICE Why?

MATT Who are you?

VOICE Why don't you just open the door?

MATT *starts to open the door, hesitates.*

VOICE Please? It's fucking cold as shit out here.

MATT *opens the door.* CHRISTINA *stands in the entrance. She is dressed in several thin layers under a thin coat. She wears the same hat, scarf, and gloves she wore in Act I. She also carries the same baglike purse. She is very cold, shivering. She looks paler, a bit gaunt, perhaps thinner.*

CHRISTINA Thanks. It looks like someone broke the window to the fire escape.

MATT Yeah, it's been that way for almost a year now. They put plastic over it but it keeps getting ripped down.

CHRISTINA It's colder in the hall than it is outside.

MATT One of the many benefits.

CHRISTINA Benefits of what?

MATT I don't know. Of um low-income um housing, I guess.

MATT *watches her for a moment. He falls to the floor. Gathers himself, stands.*

CHRISTINA Are you all right?

MATT I'm fine. I just . . . I'm fine.

CHRISTINA . . . Can I come in?

MATT Um, sure.

He steps aside. She enters. He closes the door, turns the room light on.

CHRISTINA (*looking around the room*) So you live here?

MATT I do, yeah.

CHRISTINA It's so small.

MATT You mean cozy, right?

CHRISTINA Cozy, sure.

MATT Small is so, I don't know, reductive or whatever.
"Cozy" makes you feel like you're getting more bang for
your buck.

CHRISTINA No, it's nice. How much do you pay?

MATT Two-eighty-five a month.

CHRISTINA Cheap.

MATT Yeah, for the East Village it's not so bad. The bathroom-in-
the-hall thing can get a little tedious. And there are only two
outlets so you develop this like emotional dependency on
extension cords, but you get used to it . . . I apologize in
advance about the heat. It goes out like every other day, thus
augmenting is necessary.

CHRISTINA I can't get over how small it is.

MATT It actually has its benefits. Keeps things simple. Prevents
you from buying too much shit. It's sort of like a return to
campus housing, but without the RA's . . . And the
overqualified maintenance crew . . . And the um good-looking
Banana Republic chicks . . .

CHRISTINA Are all these books yours?

MATT Yeah. I like having them around me. Makes it feel like less
of a POW torture chamber.

CHRISTINA You've read them all?

MATT Most of them. Except for the Curious George omnibus.
Totally impenetrable and overblown . . .

Awkward pause.

CHRISTINA (*extending her hand*) I'm Christine.

MATT Um, I already know you.

CHRISTINA You do?

MATT Yes, actually.

CHRISTINA (*retracting her hand*) Oh. We've met?

MATT You could say that, yeah. Except last time I was um *introduced* to you, you were using the name Christin*a*. With like an "a" on the end. I assume that's a variation.

CHRISTINA I prefer Christine.

MATT What, like depending on what side of the Atlantic you're on? . . . You seriously don't remember me?

CHRISTINA I'm sorry, lately my memory sucks. Where did we . . . ?

MATT What, *meet*?

CHRISTINA Yeah. Was it in Paris? Or, wait, are you that guy I sat with on the train to Copenhagen? The guy with the thumbs?

MATT No, that wasn't me.

CHRISTINA Are you sure? Because on the train to Copenhagen I sat next to this guy and he had these triple-jointed thumbs. It was creepy. He could make them like stick in these weird positions. He had a zittier face, but the resemblance is sort of uncanny . . .

MATT Um, we met in the Red Light District, actually. A year ago. At the Crown Hotel. Davis was with you in the windows or whatever you call them and brought you back to our room. The three of us hung out for a while. And then Davis left and we, well I mean you and I um—

CHRISTINA Oh. Wait. You were the *friend*.

MATT Yeah, I was the friend . . . I still am the friend. Referring to someone in the present tense can be surprisingly good for his or her self-esteem.

CHRISTINA I'm sorry.

MATT No, don't be. It's cool . . .

CHRISTINA What's your name again—Colin?

MATT Colin?

CHRISTINA Yeah, Colin.

MATT Like Copenhagen Colin?

CHRISTINA Come on, seriously. It's Colin, right? Or something
like that.

MATT *doesn't respond.*

CHRISTINA Brian?

MATT *doesn't respond.*

CHRISTINA Clarke.

MATT *doesn't respond.*

CHRISTINA Milt.

MATT You're getting warmer.

CHRISTINA Shit.

MATT Matt.

CHRISTINA Matt, right.

MATT *Milt?*

CHRISTINA I had the *M* right.

MATT Do I look like a fucking *Milt?*

CHRISTINA No, you look like a Colin . . . I'm kidding. You look
like a Matt.

Awkward pause.

MATT Here, sit down.

He wipes the dust off of his desk chair. She sits.

CHRISTINA Matt, right. You were the one who . . .

MATT Who what?

CHRISTINA No, nothing. I just remember you had that problem.
   With your kidneys or something.

He grabs a milk crate next to his small refrigerator, sets it down, sits.

MATT It was my um intestines, actually.

CHRISTINA That's right. You had some sort of disease.

MATT Bacteria infection.

CHRISTINA And you wouldn't drop acid.

MATT Smoke pot.

CHRISTINA Right, you wouldn't smoke any pot because you
   were like all depressed and on Prozac or something.

MATT Actually, I *was* sort of depressed at the time. But the drug I
   was on is called Flagyl. And it's an antibiotic. I had this thing
   called giardia.

CHRISTINA Oh, shit—that was *you?*

MATT Yeah, that was me—the sexy giardia guy.

CHRISTINA Wow. That's so weird, right?

Awkward pause.

CHRISTINA . . . So how've you been?

MATT I've been good. Pretty good, yeah.

CHRISTINA Good. Your bowel problems are behind you, I'm
   assuming.

MATT Intestinal. Yeah, they're pretty much behind me. In more
   ways than one . . . How've you been?

CHRISTINA I've been good.

MATT Cool.

CHRISTINA Hey, didn't you used to wear glasses?

MATT Glasses? No.

CHRISTINA Are you sure? Like those little round ones?

MATT I've never worn glasses. I'm sure people *think* of me as wearing glasses. I mean, I'm not exactly what you'd call the like Lorenzo Lamas of the East Village or whatever, but I'm proud to say that throughout my thirty-one-year reign as King of Nerdville I have miraculously managed to remain ophthalmologically unchallenged.

CHRISTINA There's something about you that's different . . . Is your hair longer or something?

MATT No, my hair's pretty much the same. I might've put on a little weight. When I met you I had just lost like twenty pounds. Because of my um . . .

CHRISTINA Bacteria problem?

MATT Yeah, that.

CHRISTINA No, now I remember—it's totally coming back to me. You were still sort of—

MATT Convalescing?

CHRISTINA Exactly. You and Davis were traveling together. You guys were in Paris and then you came to Amsterdam. You're an actor.

MATT Writer.

CHRISTINA That's right. You were working on some article.

MATT Play.

CHRISTINA I mean play. It was about a train wreck, right?

MATT Well, sort of, but not really.

CHRISTINA No, it was about a train wreck, I'm almost positive. It had "geese" in the title.

MATT Birds.

CHRISTINA I mean, birds.

MATT It was called *Speckled Birds*.

CHRISTINA Yeah, *The Speckled Bird*.

MATT *Speckled Birds*. In the plural. And no *The*.

CHRISTINA Sorry.

MATT No, don't be. I just have this like neurotic, control-freak
thing with titles. I'm sort of anti-article. No *A*'s or *An*'s or *The*'s.
The article in the title is so, I don't know, like Ernest
Hemingway or something.

She takes her hat off.

CHRISTINA Did you ever finish it?

MATT What, *Speckled Birds*? No.

CHRISTINA Why not?

MATT I don't know. I guess I sort of got like derailed.

CHRISTINA Oh.

MATT But I started something new. Single set. Three characters.
Lights up, lights down—that kind of thing.

CHRISTINA Well that's cool.

MATT Yeah, with playwriting there's lots of false starts. Ill-fated
first acts, etcetera. I blame it all on Shakespeare. He stole all
my ideas like three hundred years before I was even born. He
futuristically ruined my career . . . (*Standing now.*) Hey, would
you like some tea or something?

CHRISTINA You don't have any coffee, do you?

MATT No, I can't do coffee. I mean, I could totally go out and get
you some if you want. Ever since the episode—

CHRISTINA With your intestines?

MATT Yeah, I sort of try and steer clear of all the major diuretics
now. I can't even look at apple juice. Tea's easier on my . . .

CHRISTINA Intestines?

MATT If I hear that word again I'll probably turn into some like genitally void Nerf puppet.

CHRISTINA Sorry.

MATT But seriously, if you want, I'll totally brave the elements and go out and ferry you a Frappuccino. There's this whole like constellation of Starbucks within a five-block radius.

CHRISTINA No, tea is good. Thanks, though.

MATT All I have is Earl Grey. Is that okay?

CHRISTINA It's fine.

MATT *crosses to the kitchenette, fills a tea kettle with water, starts the portable stove top, prepares teabags in mugs, etc.*

MATT So where'd you fly in from?

CHRISTINA Paris.

MATT How was it?

CHRISTINA I slept through most of it. But it was weird. When we started circling over JFK they almost wouldn't land the plane because of all the snow.

MATT Yeah, it was coming down pretty hard earlier. We're supposed to get another big storm tonight. Like multiple inches . . . You flying back out tomorrow?

CHRISTINA No, why?

MATT Oh, no reason. It's just that before I let you in you said you were passing through town.

CHRISTINA I am.

MATT Where you heading?

CHRISTINA I was gonna take a train to go visit my parents.

MATT They're in Baltimore, right?

CHRISTINA How did you know that?

MATT You told me. Back in um . . . when we met.

CHRISTINA I told you *that*?

MATT You did, yes.

CHRISTINA That's weird.

MATT The whole night was sort of weird, actually.

CHRISTINA What else did I tell you?

MATT How you were going to Bard and wound up staying in Paris when you were studying abroad your sophomore year. And how you were performing at some bar in the Latin Quarter and you met this gay lawyer with dual Dutch and French citizenship who you wound up marrying because he gave you a lot of money or whatever and you spent X amount of months doing your thing in Amsterdam and X amount of months like posing as his wife in Paris.

CHRISTINA I wasn't posing as his wife. I was his wife.

MATT Oh, right. But he was gay, so it was sort of an act, right?

CHRISTINA A marriage is a marriage.

Awkward pause.

MATT You also told me about how you used to be an actress. And that the last play you were in was some postmodern version of *Oklahoma* that was set in a lawn-mower repair shop and everyone was half bionic or had like Duracell batteries sticking out of their backs or something.

CHRISTINA Wow. You know a lot of shit about me.

MATT I could go on and on, actually. I have a memory like a . . . very nerdy elephant.

CHRISTINA I remember your play and your chlamydia—

MATT Giardia.

CHRISTINA Yeah, that. For some reason I can remember that stuff really clearly . . . but other things . . .

MATT I came in like point four seconds. I think it's a safe bet to
    assume that it wasn't one of your most unforgettable
    experiences, Christina.
CHRISTINA Christine.
MATT I mean Christine. I'd be willing to like mortgage my books
    on that. Well, if you could actually mortgage books . . . I
    hadn't been with a woman in over three years. I don't blame
    you for not remembering.

Awkward pause.

CHRISTINA So have you been with anyone else?
MATT What, since I was with you? Of course.
CHRISTINA Really?
MATT Yeah, why?
CHRISTINA You just looked left. When people look left it means
    they're lying.
MATT According to who?
CHRISTINA I learned it from an old acting teacher.
MATT And which way do they look when they're telling the truth.
CHRISTINA Up.

MATT *looks left. He looks up.*

MATT So I totally just lied. But it's a choice.
CHRISTINA To be celibate?
MATT Sort of, yeah.
CHRISTINA Keeps things simple?
MATT Yeah, simple, sure . . . So you're on your way to Baltimore?
CHRISTINA My train leaves tomorrow, yeah.
MATT Where are you staying? Tonight, I mean.

CHRISTINA I'm not sure yet.

MATT Well, you're more than welcome to . . . I mean it's not
    exactly the St. Regis, but . . .

CHRISTINA Thanks.

MATT How long will you be down there?

CHRISTINA Sort of indefinitely. It depends, I guess.

MATT On what.

CHRISTINA On a lot.

The tea kettle starts to whistle. MATT *crosses to it, turns it off. He pours
the boiling water into the mugs.*

MATT Milk or honey?

CHRISTINA No thanks.

MATT *crosses back to* CHRISTINA, *hands her a mug of tea, then
realizes he has forgotten to give her anything to set it on and gives
her some random paperback novel as a saucer. He then sits on the
end of the bed. They sit in silence for a moment, warming their
hands.*

CHRISTINA You wouldn't happen to have a cigarette, would you?

MATT I don't smoke . . . That was Davis.

CHRISTINA *sips her tea.*

MATT So, how long has it been?

CHRISTINA Since what?

MATT Since you were on this side of the pond.

CHRISTINA Almost six years.

MATT Whoa.

CHRISTINA What?

MATT Nothing. It's just . . . Well, that's a long time to be away.

CHRISTINA Yeah, I was gonna come back a few times, but I sort of got sucked into performing. And then 9/11 happened . . . And then I got married.

MATT Are you close to your parents?

CHRISTINA Not really.

MATT You don't stay in touch?

CHRISTINA We did for the first year or so. But they were pretty pissed that I quit school.

MATT Do you have any brothers or sisters?

CHRISTINA No.

MATT Is that going to be like weird?

CHRISTINA What.

MATT To see your parents?

CHRISTINA It will be, yes.

MATT Do you mind me asking why you're going home?

CHRISTINA I just thought it was time.

MATT Cool.

CHRISTINA And I'm sick.

MATT Oh . . . What, like *sick* sick?

CHRISTINA Yeah.

MATT Should I not ask?

CHRISTINA I have AIDS.

MATT Oh. Shit . . . Wow, I'm really sorry, Christina. I mean Christine.

She starts to cry. MATT *is paralyzed for a moment, but manages to move to her. He comforts her awkwardly. After a minute, he quickly crosses to the kitchen and seizes a roll of paper towels. He tears off a few sheets, crosses back to* CHRISTINA, *hands them to her.*

CHRISTINA Thanks.

She wipes her face, blows her nose.

CHRISTINA I can't believe I'm fucking crying.
MATT No, totally cry all you want. There's plenty of Bounty.

*He awkwardly comforts her again for a moment, attempts to touch her
face but retracts his hand, then grabs a garbage can instead, setting it
next to her for easy paper-towel disposal.*

MATT How long have you known?
CHRISTINA About a month.
MATT Jesus. You must be . . .
CHRISTINA Yeah.
MATT People live a long time with it now. I mean they have all of
    these new treatments, right?
CHRISTINA I guess. But you have to be able to afford them.
MATT What about your husband?
CHRISTINA What about him?
MATT Can't he help you?
CHRISTINA He won't.
MATT But isn't he like legally responsible?
CHRISTINA He was, yeah.
MATT I mean, what happened to "for better and for worse" and
    all that?
CHRISTINA It was too embarrassing for him. He divorced me
    on grounds of adultery. Things got ugly and I lost my work
    permit.
MATT You told your husband you were sick and he turned you out?
CHRISTINA After I got the results I went to his firm to tell him
    and he started making calls right there at his desk.
MATT What a fucking asshole.

CHRISTINA I don't blame him, really. I mean, who wants a
    fucking trophy wife with AIDS?
MATT But still. That's so, I don't know . . . low . . . Do you know
    how you got it?
CHRISTINA No.
MATT Don't you have protected sex?
CHRISTINA I always make my partners wear condoms.
MATT Did you ever have like a blood transfusion?
CHRISTINA No. The only thing I can think of is I did heroin a
    few times with this guy from Zurich but the needles were in
    these fucking hermetically sealed packets . . . I don't know how
    I got it. That doesn't even matter. The fact is I got it.
MATT How did you find out?
CHRISTINA At a routine checkup at my gynecologist.
MATT Do you have any money?
CHRISTINA I used my last three hundred dollars getting here.
MATT What's your plan for Baltimore?
CHRISTINA I'm just gonna get on the train.
MATT That's illegal, Christina.
CHRISTINA Christine.
MATT I mean Christine. The fucking Amtrak police will totally
    throw you off the train. Can't your parents wire you some cash?
CHRISTINA I haven't spoken to them in over five years.
MATT So now would be a pretty good time, don't you think? I
    mean, you're not calling to like ask to borrow the car or
    something . . . Can't you get treated in Paris?
CHRISTINA Albert and I weren't married long enough for me to
    get full citizenship. So I lost my medical eligibility.
MATT But they can't refuse you treatment, can they? I mean, they
    wouldn't throw you out on the street.
CHRISTINA I just felt like I needed to come back.

CHRISTINA *rises and crosses to the kitchen, stares out the window. The phone rings.* MATT *doesn't answer it. It rings twice and then his answering machine picks up.*

MATT'S VOICE Hey, it's Matt. Please leave a message. (*A beep.*)
DAVIS'S VOICE Yo, Matt, it's me. I think I left my cell phone over there last night. I'm heading downtown to meet Sarah later and I was wondering if I could stop by to pick it up. If you get this message, give me a call on my land line. All right, bro. Hope the writing's going well. I'll see you later.

The answering machine beeps again. A silence.

CHRISTINA That was Davis, wasn't it?
MATT Yeah, actually, it was.
CHRISTINA Are you gonna call him back?
MATT Not right now.
CHRISTINA You should call him back. I mean he needs his phone, right?
MATT He'll probably stop by.

She crosses to her purse, sits in the chair.

MATT Look, Christina—
CHRISTINA Christine.
MATT I mean Christine. I'd like to help you.
CHRISTINA How?
MATT I don't know. I only have a few hundred dollars in the bank but I'll totally get you that train ticket. It can't be more than fifty bucks.
CHRISTINA It's seventy.

MATT Fine. Seventy bucks, that's nothing. We'll go to Penn
    Station together. I'll put you on the train.
CHRISTINA I'd feel weird taking your money.
MATT You can't afford not to. Look, you don't even have to pay
    me back. It's only seventy dollars. I just started this temp job
    that pays like twenty bucks an hour. And as far as having a
    place to stay tonight, you can totally crash here. I have this like
    polystyrenc yoga mat thing. I can sleep on the floor.
CHRISTINA (*half joking*) What, you don't want to sleep with me?
MATT No, I totally want to sleep with you, Christina. I mean
    Christine. I just . . . I don't know . . . I think you should be
    comfortable, that's all.

CHRISTINA *hands the paper towels back to* MATT.

CHRISTINA Would you mind if I took a shower?
MATT Not at all. It's in the hall. There's a clean towel on the shelf
    in the closet.

She rises. He does as well, crossing to the kitchen to give her some space.
He might put something in a cupboard. Hanging on the inside of the
closet door is CHRISTINA*'s red dress from the end of Act I. She has to*
move the chair to enter the closet and doesn't see it until she comes out
with the towel. She closes the door. She is suddenly lightheaded, has to
sit on the bed.

MATT You okay?
CHRISTINA I'm fine. I'm just a little lightheaded. It was a long
    flight.

She stands.

MATT Have you like eaten?

CHRISTINA I couldn't eat the plane food.

MATT You must be starving. Maybe I should go get something.

CHRISTINA Not yet.

MATT Oh. Why?

CHRISTINA Wait till I finish my shower.

MATT Okay.

CHRISTINA I'd feel safer.

MATT Then I'll totally stay right here . . . The shower's um down
    the hall to your left.

CHRISTINA Thanks.

MATT Sure.

She turns and exits. As soon as the door is shut, MATT *spots Davis's cell
phone next to a lamp. He opens it, shuts it.*

A knock on the door. MATT *puts the cell phone back.*

CHRISTINA'S VOICE It's me.

MATT *opens the door.*

CHRISTINA Can I borrow some soap and shampoo?

MATT Of course.

MATT *hands her a large bucket containing shower supplies.*

MATT It takes a minute for the hot water to kick in.

CHRISTINA Hey, thanks again.

MATT You're welcome.

CHRISTINA You're really sweet.

MATT I, well, um, thanks. Thank you.

She turns and exits down the hall. MATT *shuts the door, turns, and in a whirlwind panic he kicks drifts of laundry under his bed, removes his sweater, replaces it with a clean shirt, throws things away, deodorizes the room with Febreze spray—he Febrezes just about everything in sight—attempts to straighten up the kitchen and wave the heat from the space heater into the room. He then quickly goes to the cupboard, removes a toothbrush and a tube of toothpaste, brushes his teeth in the sink with Olympic velocity, smells his armpits, reaches back into the cupboard, removes some deodorant, applies it very quickly, checks his reflection in the mirror, fixes his hair, puts a baseball hat on, takes it off, and then almost passes out. He sits on the bed for a moment, almost starts to cry. He tries to make himself stop by punching his leg repeatedly. He stops crying.* MATT *then seizes the phone. He dials, waits.*

MATT (*into phone*) Hey, Davis, it's me. I um got your message. You might not get this, but what I wanted to say was that yeah, you did leave your cell phone over here. It's on my bookcase, actually. But tonight might not be the best time to come over. I mean, you can totally give it a shot but I'll most likely be out. I've been sort of feeling cooped up lately and I was thinking about going to check out a movie. So tomorrow might be better. All right . . . Hey, Sarah. Later.

He hangs up, spots CHRISTINA's *bag, crosses to it, opens it, removes the snow globe that* DAVIS *had given* CHRISTINA *back in Amsterdam.* MATT *shakes it, stares at it for a moment, then puts it back in her bag.*

Suddenly, MATT *seizes the phone again, dials, waits.*

MATT (*into phone*) Hey, Davis, it's me again. I just wanted to let you know that I decided that I'm definitely gonna go check out a movie. I mean I'm just sitting here, waiting for the snow . . . again. So don't waste your time stopping by. I'll give you a call tomorrow.

MATT *hangs up, then turns to* CHRISTINA*'s bag again. He fixes it so that it doesn't look tampered with.* CHRISTINA *reenters. Her hair is wet and she is dressed in the same clothes.*

MATT Was there any hot water?
CHRISTINA Uh-huh.
MATT No shower-room floor surprises? At least once a week someone leaves this totally unnameable like supple mass in the corner . . .

He watches her for a moment.

CHRISTINA What.
MATT Nothing. You're just so pretty.

Awkward pause.

MATT You can hang the towel on the hook on the door.

She hangs the towel. He takes the bucket from her, puts it away. She crosses to her purse.

MATT Here, take the bed.

She sits on the bed. He sets the afghan beside her. She puts her hat on. He then positions the space heater so that it is closer to her, waves some heat toward her.

ADAM RAPP

MATT You look like Jean Seberg. With your hair under your hat like that.

CHRISTINA Who's that?

MATT Oh my god, you don't know who Jean Seberg is?

CHRISTINA No.

MATT She was an American actress who starred in this 1960 French New Wave film called *Breathless*. It was directed by Jean-Luc Godard and written by François Truffaut. In French it's called *À bout de souffle*. It's an amazing movie. Like one of those ones that change your life or whatever. Jean Seberg played this sort of lost American girl living in Paris who's in love with this car thief, Michel. Michel is played by Jean-Paul Belmondo and he's this like total Humphrey Bogart wannabe, but in a cool way. All they do is steal cars and make love, but Michel shoots this cop and then they're fucked and they try to escape to Italy. In 1983 they did this cheesy American remake with like Richard Gere. It was set in Vegas instead of Paris and they're trying to get to L.A. instead of Italy. It was sort of an all time low in American filmmaking.

   Jean Seberg didn't wear a hat but she had short hair. The legend goes that after she had starred in these two flops, *Saint Joan* and this other French film called *Bonjour tristesse*, Godard like saw her at a café in Paris and got all spellbound and asked her to be in his movie. She was originally from Marshalltown, Iowa . . . She was really beautiful so it's like a high compliment.

CHRISTINA Thanks.

MATT I can't believe you don't know that film. After *Breathless* came out, like hundreds of thousands of women cut their hair short. She totally inspired this whole new look. She was married four times. Later she sort of freaked out and moved to L.A. and joined the Black Panthers. Some people believe that the FBI was actually after her. When she was forty-one she like OD'd on barbiturates. They found her dead in a Paris suburb.

CHRISTINA So did it change your life?

MATT What—*Breathless*?

CHRISTINA Yeah.

MATT Not really. I mean it definitely *should* have. I'll probably go see it again at some point. This theater in the West Village revives it every so often.

Pause.

CHRISTINA So what's your new play about?

MATT You really want to know?

CHRISTINA I do, yes.

MATT It's actually about two friends who go to Amsterdam. They both sleep with the same um girl.

CHRISTINA And what happens?

MATT Well, one of them sort of falls in love with her and he can't seem to get over it.

CHRISTINA Is the girl—

MATT She's a prostitute, yeah.

CHRISTINA I was actually gonna ask if she's in love with one of them.

MATT Oh. She is. But not with the right one. One of them is a bit quiet and nerdy, and the other one is sort of dickish and macho. The quiet, nerdy one is in love with her but he isn't really her type. And the dickish, macho one *is* her type, but he's not interested in her. At some point the dickish, macho one gives her this like Fabergé glass egg thing that changes colors—it's sort of like a mood egg. He buys it as a joke and sort of unloads it on her because he can't fit it in his suitcase and she takes it the wrong way.

CHRISTINA She thinks it actually means something.

MATT She does sort of, yeah.

CHRISTINA That's sad.

MATT It is sad. But it's funny too. In like a sad way.

CHRISTINA How does it end?

MATT Well, you see, that's the part that's screwing me up. I'm like three-quarters of the way through it and the double unrequited love thing totally works but I can't figure out the final movement. The hypotenuse of the love triangle never quite gets completed because they're all like star-crossed or whatever. And beyond that, it's not conventionally structured because there are these like songs in it that sort of come out of nowhere. Not to say that there isn't at least some semblance of organic logic at work. The female character used to be this famous torch singer in Istanbul. Sometimes to communicate she has no recourse but to sing. And other times she functions as this like five-a.m. vision in the quiet, nerdy guy's head. Don't get me wrong, it's not a musical. And it's not like Brechtian or whatever. It's just what it is. I mean, what it definitely *isn't* is your typical Aristotelian, three-act, architecturally sound type of thing. It's not what they call a well-made play. It's more of this like half-remembered dream or a spell or a *haunting* or something. If anything it's an *unwell*-made play. And my instincts are to let it sort of fade out; to like resist the big clichéd, melodramatic ending. (*Sitting on the bed now.*) But I keep writing into this like weird corner of confrontation and emotional apocalypse. Where the girl and the quiet nerdy guy who she doesn't love wind up alone and like go round and round about why they should and shouldn't be together and then peace is achieved after some totally cheesy song about mermaids trapped under calving icebergs or whatever.

CHRISTINA And all of this happens in Amsterdam?

MATT In Amsterdam, yeah. In one night. Lights up, lights down. But real life never works like that, right? . . . I mean it really doesn't, right?

CHRISTINA Maybe you should just let it fade out like you said.

MATT Maybe.

Awkward pause.

MATT I'm not writing an act break into it. I don't think the audience should be let off the hook. But these days everyone wants an intermission so they can sell shit. Like chocolate-covered espresso beans and thirty-dollar T-shirts with pictures of Tony Kushner eating a banana.

A silence.

MATT I better go get us some food.

He crosses to his winter coat, starts to put it on.

CHRISTINA Hey, Mark?

MATT Matt.

CHRISTINA I mean Matt. Sorry.

MATT What.

CHRISTINA Why are you being so nice to me?

MATT Look, Christine or Christina or whatever your name is, I feel I have to say something. And I have no idea how this is going to come out, so please don't freak out and stone me to death or kick me in the balls or like projectile vomit from boredom . . .

CHRISTINA Okay.

MATT How to start . . . Let's see . . . Um, since we were together last January I haven't been able to like stop thinking about you. I mean, it was easily one of the biggest things that's ever happened to me. I know that like sexually speaking at least it was this totally uneventful blip of antimatter for you, but I'm pretty convinced that despite my inept, like desperate sexual brevity or whatever that something real passed between us. Even if for a moment. And I know you remember it—you fucking have to—because I'd never known that feeling before. And when that kind of thing happens there has to be at least a shred of mutuality at play, even if it's like point seven percent.

You like walked out of your dress. And then you helped me take my clothes off. And then you took my hand and led me to the bed. It was . . . Well, it was more than the sex, way more than that. You were like *kind*. And it helped me. It helped me so much, Christina. In ways that I'd need like the twelve thousand semitones of dolphin language to articulate. And I'm sure that with all the guys or johns or clients or whatever you call your rotisserie of men that most of the time it's just a series of these like fast, pound-of-flesh experiences for you, but that's not what happened for me. It wasn't this like anecdote that American guys go over there to collect. They eat a few space cakes and fuck a window whore and get a tattoo of like a dagger or a yin-yang sign or a fucking stallion getting struck by lightning. That's not what it was about for me. It was way bigger than that. And it was way bigger than a play or a paperback novel or like some precious cultural artifact or whatever. It was bigger than anything I could ever fucking write about.

I mean, I spend most of my time in my head, like trapped with my own fucking terrible, spiritually corrosive thoughts.

And sure, I know a lot of people suffer and have constant nightmares and mental illness and horrible crushing madness or whatever, but for some reason, it's not easy for me. To be with those thoughts, I mean. And sometimes disappearing seems like the only fucking answer. Just like ending it, you know?

I used to wish that I could make a painting of a dog eating spaghetti or like write a haiku or a fucking play that would push those thoughts out of my head permanently, but I could never figure it out . . . But after I met you I . . . I don't know, I just felt like I could sort of be in the world again. And it made things in my head, I don't know . . . like slow down for a while. And I don't even know why. I mean I hardly know you, but at the same time I do. Something happened in that room in Amsterdam.

And I know this is going to sound like some totally New Age Carlos Castaneda psychic cookbook or something, but sometimes I close my eyes and send you thoughts. I'll be like, "Hey, Christina. I hope you're doing well. I hope everything's going good for you in that city you live in . . . Stay safe, okay? . . . I love you."

And I've been doing this thing lately where I imagine what you were like as a little girl. In Baltimore or whatever. Like flying a fucking kite or smashing chocolate cake on your coloring book or making a lemonade sign or eating crayons under the patio furniture or whatever.

CHRISTINA I never had patio furniture.

MATT So I'll nix the patio furniture. We can make it a picnic table.

CHRISTINA And my name's not Christina.

MATT So there's a vowel change. Christine's just as pretty.

CHRISTINA It's not Christine, either.

MATT Oh. Well, what is it?

CHRISTINA Annie.

MATT Annie?

She nods.

MATT So I can adjust to that . . . I suddenly feel like you should
show me your ID or something.

CHRISTINA *reaches into her bag, removes her passport, opens it. He
looks at it for a moment.*

MATT Are you really from Baltimore?

CHRISTINA Aberdeen.

MATT And you're really sick?

CHRISTINA Yes.

MATT So I'll start calling you Annie, it's a minor adjustment . . .
And I'll tell you one more thing because what the hell I've already
said too much and then I'll shut up and go get us some food.

CHRISTINA What.

MATT I sleep with your dress. The red one that you changed into
that night in Amsterdam. You left it in our room. I was going
to return it to you the next day but I couldn't. I rolled it up in a
towel and like absconded with it. I actually sleep with it,
Christina. I mean Christine. I mean Annie. Because it has this
smell. Like sesame oil and hairspray and frozen cigarettes. And
there's this faint clove thing going on too.

He starts to turn the covers of the bed down.

MATT I like tuck it into the bed every morning and—

CHRISTINA It's hanging in the closet.

MATT You're right, it is hanging in the closet. It's totally hanging there, you know why? Because I fucking put it on last night. I actually put on your red dress because I wanted to feel what it was like to be inside you again. I actually slept in it and it was like we were holding each other or like slow dancing or something. That kind of slow dancing where you hardly move and you just sort of lean up against each other because you need the other person that fucking bad.

   And I couldn't wait for tonight. Till I got tired. I take these pills now to help me sleep and I was going to take them earlier than usual because I couldn't wait to be inside you again. You see, because sleeping is the one thing I look forward to anymore. Because I get to be with you.

   And then tonight there's this knock on my door and here you are . . . I'm sorry, I'm totally rambling. And now my hands are like shaking. What are you hungry for anyway—you want a cheeseburger?

CHRISTINA *nods.*

MATT Cool. Anything else? Fries? A pickle?

She shakes her head. He pulls a hat out of his coat pocket, puts it on, stands there for a moment.

MATT Was that okay? All that stuff that I just spewed?
CHRISTINA Sure.
MATT Because I'm glad I told you.
CHRISTINA Me too.
MATT So I'll be right back . . . Are you gonna be okay?

She nods.

MATT Are you warm enough?

She nods.

MATT Cool. Then I'll just go then.

MATT *crosses to the front door, starts to open the door, stops, turns back.*

MATT So don't um like leave, okay?

MATT *exits.*

CHRISTINA *removes the afghan and crosses to his makeshift closet. She opens the closet door, removes the red dress, pulls it off its hanger, stares at it for a moment. Then she undresses, puts the dress on, crosses to the kitchen, uses the small mirror to fix her hair. She pinches her cheeks to give some color to her face. She stands before the mirror for a long moment.*

There is a knock at the door. A MALE VOICE *can be heard.*

VOICE Matt?

More knocking.

VOICE Hey, Matt! . . . Come on. Wake up, nerd, I need my cell.

Suddenly, the door flies open kung-fu style. DAVIS *is standing in the entrance. He is wearing nice clothes, a good leather jacket.*

DAVIS Hi.

CHRISTINA *stands there.*

DAVIS Is Matt around?

She shakes her head. He enters, closes the door.

DAVIS He's not?

She shakes her head.

DAVIS Really.

She nods.

DAVIS Do you know where he is?

She shakes her head.

DAVIS Was he here earlier?

She nods.

DAVIS How long ago did he leave?

She holds up ten fingers.

DAVIS Ten minutes ago?

She nods.

DAVIS What are you supposed to be, like a prom mime or
    something?

CHRISTINA (*with a French accent, from now on*) He just left.

DAVIS Oh. Is he coming back?

CHRISTINA I think he is, yes.

DAVIS Do I know you?

CHRISTINA We met last winter.

DAVIS We did? Where?

CHRISTINA Amsterdam.

DAVIS Oh. Really?

CHRISTINA You don't remember?

DAVIS I don't, no. I mean, I met a lot of people in Amsterdam.

CHRISTINA Well, I remember you very well.

DAVIS Wait, were you that guide at the Anne Frank museum?
The one in the corduroy jumpsuit who kept calling the attic a
fucking garret?

CHRISTINA No.

DAVIS You sure?

CHRISTINA I am positive.

DAVIS Oh, wait a minute. Fuck me with a curling iron, you're
that chick who threw a plate of Swedish pancakes at me.

CHRISTINA No.

DAVIS Yes.

CHRISTINA No.

DAVIS Yeah. Because I called you a Dutch cunt.

CHRISTINA I'm not Dutch.

DAVIS No, I know. You're actually from Brussels or you're like
Czech or Hungarian or something. But I called you a Dutch
cunt and you threw that plate of Swedish pancakes at me and
this very menstrual-looking Rorschach of strawberry sauce
went all over this gabardine cowboy shirt I bought in Spain.
Later we made out in the bathroom of that café with all those
Marx Brothers pictures on the walls. Groucho's or Harpo's or
fucking Flippo's or whatever it was called.

CHRISTINA I met you at the windows.

DAVIS Oh. You mean you're that whore?

CHRISTINA Yes.

DAVIS No shit?

CHRISTINA Christina.

DAVIS Yeah, Christina. Matt fucked you.

CHRISTINA So did you.

DAVIS Did I?

CHRISTINA Yes.

DAVIS Really? Wow. I must have been really fucking stoned or something because I can't place it. Was I good? Just kidding. Um, I actually came by to grab my cell phone. I don't have to have some like international Frog search warrant to get by, do I?

He crosses to the kitchen, starts hunting, grabs the milk that MATT *had left out for tea, sniffs at it, drinks a slug.*

DAVIS So how are you? *Comment allez-vous? Ça va bien?*

CHRISTINA I'm good, thank you. And you?

DAVIS I'm fucking happy as a handshake. Just trying to beat the snow. We're in for a pretty big storm tonight . . . (*Crossing to the mini-fridge with the milk.*) Hey, do you ever get snow in Amsterdam?

CHRISTINA Sometimes, yes. But it . . . how do you say— disappears?

DAVIS Melts?

CHRISTINA Yes. It melts very quickly. And the channels rarely freeze.

From the mini-fridge he removes a squeezable bottle of ketchup, removes the milk cap, squeezes some ketchup into the milk, puts the milk cap back on, sets the milk and the ketchup back in the mini-fridge.

DAVIS   Yeah, I can't quite imagine anyone ice skating there.
Stoners on skates.

DAVIS *moves to the bed. From a crate he flings a few pairs of underwear
behind him. He looks under the bed. He sifts through* MATT's *various
piles of things.*

DAVIS   So how long are you in New York for?
CHRISTINA   Not long.
DAVIS   Just passing through?
CHRISTINA   Yes.
DAVIS   Business or pleasure?
CHRISTINA   Pleasure.
DAVIS   *Plaisir.* Hey, if you're looking for clients I have a couple of
lonely friends I could probably set you up with. Big beefy guys
with bad hair. Smart fuckers, though.
CHRISTINA   No thank you.
DAVIS   *Non merci.* Are you still hooking?
CHRISTINA   No.
DAVIS   What, you had some sort of come-to-Jesus moment
or something? A little too much viscosity down low? . . .
Viscosity is this friction thing that happens in sports cars.
High engine viscosity. It's an old Quaker State commercial.
Or maybe it's Pennzoil . . . Oh, right. Wrong country.
Sorry.

DAVIS *crosses to* MATT's *desk, starts rooting through his stuff, picking
up papers, etc.*

DAVIS   Look at all this shit. Used Kleenex. Mylanta. Robitussin.
Benadryl. It's like a fucking supply depot for insomniac,
tubercular neurotics. (*Touching the books.*) *A Fan's Notes.*

Crazy Cock. Ask the fucking *Dust* . . . You know he reads the same authors over and over again? John Fante, Frederick Exley, Henry Miller. How ironic, right? I mean these guys lived crazy lives. They were these demented, alcoholic, promiscuous fucking apes who had syphilis and got crabs and fell asleep in dive bars and camped on people's sofas and Matt like cloisters off in this monastic cell like some malnourished warlock and picks lint out of his navel and stares out the window for several hours a day. You'd think he'd take a little stock in his heroes. Let it rip every once in a while. I can't even get him to go to the fucking movies with me anymore.

CHRISTINA Maybe he is just shy.

DAVIS Maybe he's just a big fucking pussy who thinks too much. The guy needs to stop living in his head. He's really starting to lose touch.

DAVIS *crosses back to the kitchen, takes a clean dishrag, stuffs it down his pants, puts it back on the kitchen counter.*

DAVIS So how'd you track him down, anyway?

CHRISTINA It was a mistake.

DAVIS Oh yeah? How's that?

CHRISTINA I was looking for you.

DAVIS Really?

CHRISTINA Yes.

DAVIS I don't get it.

CHRISTINA In Amsterdam I asked for your address.

DAVIS And I gave you Matt's?

CHRISTINA Yes.

DAVIS God, I'm such a dick, right?

DAVIS *crosses back to* MATT's *desk, turns up* MATT's *computer screen, touches the touch pad. The screen is illuminated. He reads.*

DAVIS What the fuck is this freak writing now? (*Scrolling down.*) He's got some character named *Davison.* Hmmm, I wonder who that could be? (*While reading.*) So why were you looking for me, anyway—do I owe you money?
CHRISTINA I missed you.
DAVIS Davison, Matthews, and *Yildiz*? What is he writing, a fucking autobiographical klezmer musical? I can just hear the dueling accordions.

He starts to type.

CHRISTINA Do you have a cigarette?
DAVIS No.
CHRISTINA Did you quit smoking?
DAVIS No . . . Fucking things are seven bucks a pack now.

DAVIS *continues typing.* CHRISTINA *starts to gather her things. She doesn't bother putting anything on; she simply gathers them in her arms and starts for the door.*

DAVIS Walrus.

CHRISTINA *stops dead in her tracks.* DAVIS *then reaches into his jacket pocket, removes a pack of cigarettes, offers her one. She sets her things down by the door, crosses to him, accepts the cigarette. He produces a lighter, lights her. He takes one for himself, lights it. They smoke.*

CHRISTINA What did you type?

DAVIS (*reading off the screen*) I typed Dear Matt-slash-Matthews, comma, If you're going to use the platform of your art to lampoon your friends, comma, perhaps it's high time to revisit your chosen vocation, full stop. I would be happy to take some Polaroids of myself in a Speedo, comma, pubes a-bursting, comma, so you can hang them on the door of your two-and-a-half-foot refrigerator, full stop. This way you wouldn't have to write an entire eighty-four-page play in order to make an ass of your best friend, full stop. You might also want to get a little craftier with your character names, full stop. Quote, Davison, unquote, and quote, Matthews, unquote, is about as subtle as an erect horse cock bobbing along the cliffs of the Costa Brava, full stop. Also, comma, your dialogue is starting to sort of suck, full stop. I would advise revisiting some Eugene O'Neill, comma, or might I recommend William Inge, comma, or even Li'l Abner, full stop. Return, return. Yours in editorial sleuthing, comma, return, return, Davis-slash-Davison, return, return. P.S., full stop. I deleted a few lines that sucked, full stop. And I found my cell phone, full stop.

He lowers the laptop screen.

DAVIS Pretty good, right?
CHRISTINA (*almost losing the accent*) Why do you pretend to be so cruel?
DAVIS What?
CHRISTINA You're not a cruel person.
DAVIS Really.
CHRISTINA You are kind and I know this to be true.
DAVIS You do, do you?
CHRISTINA Yes.

ADAM RAPP

DAVIS Interesting.

CHRISTINA You are only sad.

DAVIS I'm sad? What is this, some sort of Christian Youth Group intervention?

CHRISTINA *goes into her purse bag, removes the globe he had given her during their first encounter. He crosses to her.*

DAVIS What's that? (*Taking it from her.*) Yeah, this is that piece of shit I bought at that knickknack shop in Paris. I didn't feel like taking it on the plane. That shop was brilliant. They had like David Hasselhoff action-figure dolls with bulges.

CHRISTINA You are not a cruel person, Davis.

DAVIS What, you think you know me?

CHRISTINA I do, yes.

DAVIS Well, I'll tell you something, Chiquita or Chitaqua or whatever your name—

CHRISTINA Christina.

DAVIS I'll tell you something, *Christina.* You're an idiot. You think you know me because I let you teabag my nuts for a few minutes? Because I stuck my finger up your ass while I fucked you like the whore you are?

CHRISTINA We made love.

DAVIS *We made love.* I was fucking bored and I felt sorry for you!

He drops the snow globe in the trash. She turns away, then turns back to him, her fists clenched.

DAVIS Oh, what. You're gonna hit me? . . . Go ahead. Hit me.

She suddenly hugs him, holding on for dear life. He pushes her to the floor. She comes back to him, trying to kiss him. He stops her, pushes her away. She tries again. He seizes her arm, a momentary struggle, and then he pulls her close and they begin making out, which moves to the bed. It is very passionate for a moment. They are both aroused and relieved. She kisses him. He turns away. She kisses him again.

After a moment, DAVIS *pulls her off the bed, sweeps the books off of* MATT's *desk, turns her around, hikes her dress up, and folds her over* MATT's *desk. He takes his pants down, spits in his hand, rubs her, and starts to take her from behind. They both get lost in it. It might be the best and worst thing they've ever felt.*

After several thrusts, DAVIS's *cell phone rings. Still inside* CHRISTINA, DAVIS *covers her mouth and answers his cell.*

DAVIS Hi honey . . . Yeah . . . Yeah . . . I'm over at Matt's . . . Yeah, I just got it. I left it on his bookshelf. He probably used up all my minutes, the little leech . . . Oh, I'm a little out of breath, I just ran up the stairs. I'll meet you there in about twenty minutes . . . I love you, too.

DAVIS *hangs up, uncovers her mouth. She is devastated. He thrusts a few more times, comes, stays inside her for a moment, and then pulls out. He pulls his pants up, stands there for a long moment.* CHRISTINA *remains folded over* MATT's *desk, her face down.*

DAVIS Well, that was weird . . . (*Using the afghan to wipe his hands.*) I should probably go wash my dick, right? . . . That was a joke . . . So I better go . . . If you see Matt, tell him I came by . . . Are you okay?

She doesn't respond.

DAVIS I didn't hurt you, did I?

She doesn't respond.

DAVIS Cool . . . I'm not a good person, Christina.

She doesn't respond.

DAVIS Well, good luck then. *Bon suar. Au revoir.*

DAVIS *exits, closing the door.*

CHRISTINA *slowly lifts herself off the desk, sits in the chair, in shock. She spots her old portable cassette player, presses a button. Tom Waits's "Jitterbug Boy" plays. She listens. Just as he starts singing, she presses Stop, sits in silence. She then spots the bottle of sleeping pills, considers them for a moment, takes them in her hand, and then rises off the chair, crosses to the door, her dress half zipped, opens the door, exits toward the fire escape, leaving the door open. In the window we can see that it has started to snow.*

Moments later, MATT *enters, carrying a few deli bags of groceries and takeout food. He sets the groceries down on the milk crate, looks around the room. He opens the door, exits to the shower room. Moments later, we see him quickly pass by the doorway, toward the fire escape. He re-enters, closes the door, and crosses to the closet, opens it, stares at the hanger that was holding the dress, removes his hat. After a moment, he slowly crosses to the desk and sits. He presses a button on the portable cassette player. Tom Waits's "Jitterbug Boy" resumes from where* CHRISTINA *had stopped it. Lights fade as the snow falls across the window.*